# THE MORNING
# OF HER DAY

The story of Mary Morgan,
hanged in Wales in 1805
for the murder of her
bastard child

by

## Jennifer Green

First published in 1987 by Divine Books
This edition 1990
by Darf Publishers Ltd,
50 Hans Crescent
London SW1X 0NA

c   Jennifer Green

ISBN 1 85077 221 5

Cover design by Sue Sharples
Typeset by Christine Morgan

Printed in Great Britain by
BPCC Wheatons Ltd, Exeter

# THE AUTHOR

Jennifer Green was born in Farnborough, Hampshire in 1938, one of six children. From a working class background, and a basic education she entered the WRNS attached to the Fleet Air Arm. Leaving the Service, her career progressed in the 1960s through mechanical engineering before holding a senior position in University administration. A further change of direction took her into executive management at the Family Planning Association, during which time her already developing beliefs in women's rights became of greater significance in her everyday life.

Ever ready for a new challenge, the early 70's presented the opportunity to set up a major Arts complex from an 18th Century listed mansion at South Hill Park, Berkshire. This was followed by six months in New Zealand researching the Arts. On her return, she undertook directing Community Services in Hampshire and in 1976 she departed for Mid Wales. In time, she took up an appointment at the Royal National College for the Blind in Hereford.

She now works as Warden of Walsingham Lodge in South West London and divides her time between there and her house in Somerset where she is working on her next book. Her main interests include public and after dinner speaking and watching cricket.

THIS BOOK IS DEDICATED TO
GLADYS GREEN
MY MOTHER AND MY FRIEND

\*\*\*\*\*\*\*\*\*\*\*\*

Some towns write their history in books.
Presteigne has written its history upon its
gravestones and, having done so, offers them
up for examination.

This book is not intended to be an exact
historical documentation; it is an honest
attempt to clear the name of a seventeen year
old servant girl, more sinned against than
sinning, and to lay my obsession with her life
until she died on the gallows in 1805.

I share this story with my good friends in
Presteigne (they know who they are) and with
Mary Morgan, who has spiritually shared my
long historical journey through her short
life.


Jennifer Green
April 1987

# CHAPTERS

In the Memory of Mary Morgan
who young and beautiful, endowed
with a good understanding and
disposition but unenlightened by the
sacred truths of Christianity became
the victim of sin and shame and
was condemned to an ignominious
death on the 11th April 1805,
for the Murder of her bastard Child

Rous'd to a first sense of guilt and
remorse by the eloquent and humane
exertions of her benevolent Judge
Mr. Justice Hardinge, she underwent
the Sentence of the Law on the
following Thursday with unfeigned
repentance and a fervent hope of
forgiveness through the merits of a
redeeming intercessor.

This Stone is erected as a merciful
appeal to the remembrance of a
departed penitent and as a remind to the
living of the frailty of human nature
when unsupported by Religion.

The gravestone erected by Judge Hardinge
Laid up in St Andrew's Church in 1982
Photograph by Anita Corbin

The Flowers on the grave of Mary Morgan;
placed there at Christmas and on the
anniversary of her death
by persons unknown.
Photograph by Anita Corbin

# CHAPTER ONE

## THE BEGINNING

At Mortimers Crossroad there is a mile stone, indicating to passers by that Ludlow lies twelve miles to the north, Hereford twenty-one miles south, that it is one hundred and forty-six miles to London and eight miles to Presteigne. London is the farthest, Presteigne the most far fetched.

The road from Mortimers Cross eases its way through the Welsh Border country with a casualness that defies urgency, almost as if to question the need for its very beginning. It bends and turns, challenging the traveller to pause, look about, and applaud the growth of history sprouting under the hedgerows, in the fertile fields and alongside the ageless river that is still tainted with the blood washed from the dead of battles past, Welsh and English alike.

The beauty of the Lugg Valley, the Black Mountains and the far distant Brecon Beacons please the eye of the beholder as the road to Presteigne winds on, past unsteady sign posts that point the way to obscure place names like Upper and Lower Lye, Wappley Hill and Byton.

A deviation from the normal route through Shobdon, over a pot-holed track safeguarded by the occasional 'sleeping policeman', leads to a former wartime air field, still sporting corrugated hangers, black sheds and a small, white, glass topped control tower that romances with World War Two. All that is needed to complete the scene are the leathercoated warriors of the air, seated in the summer sun awaiting the call to reach for the sky.

Passing through today, the silence is interrupted by the gentle buzz of the tiny planes that fly for fun, drop the parachutists and tow the gliders, that return to earth on the currents of air that rise and fall above the hill that preserves the privacy of Presteigne.

The road dips just before the Byton turn and then rises again at the junction, passing 'The Bell', a one time public house reputed to be the last in England, where in the days of the restrictive Welsh licensing laws the landlord had to cope with the secret cider drinkers of Presteigne who were keen to cross the border to indulge themselves.

It isn't far to Presteigne now and eager eyes search left and right for just the briefest glimpse of the old county township that lies hidden from present day invaders. The imposing evergreen forests and deep clefted hills stand firm, as if placed there at the request of some unknown authority, to protect the secrets history has imposed upon the living and the dead of this introverted community. And there it is, for a brief moment it appears upstream of the River Lugg, laid out in the valley and seasonally highlighted. In the spring it is encased by the green fields, in summer it is washed by the brightness of the sun, in the autumn it is shrouded in a mellow mist from bonfires and rising damp. In the winter the buildings are camouflaged by snow and identified only by the woodsmoke from the chimney pots and the glow-worm effect of the domestic lighting that breaks the darkness.

The road follows the river into town, past rich farm lands and farmers, the splendid houses of the landed gentry, and the small cottages and converted barns of the 'good life brigade'. Just before the common land a large modern sign post, emblazoned with a red dragon, bi-lingually states "Croeso I Cymru - Welcome to Wales".

I entered Presteigne from the Hereford end and I didn't know if it was me or the town that was lost. It was a chance meeting. West Wales was the original destination, a September holiday with a friend in 1971 required a stopover at some place on route. The place happened to be Presteigne, unheard of by me, briefly known to my companion and from the moment I happened upon it, the relationship between me and a seventeen year old servant girl who died in 1805 was destined to absorb my thinking and play an important, if mystifying, part in my life.

It was 6.20 pm on the town clock - it could well have been 6.20 am. The High Street appeared deserted. A few cars parked casually along one side of the road, were convincing enough to prove it was 1971 and not 1871. The only other occupant of the main highway through the town was an engaging ginger Tom cat with a battered right ear, who strolled along in the middle of the thoroughfayre with an air of complacency which showed his road sense was based upon his personal experience of the early evening traffic. Time was to make it clear that he did not give way to horsepower, horsepower gave way to him, and it wasn't long before the realisation dawned that this was standard procedure for Presteigne.

Arrival in the town coincided with opening time at 'The Bull' and all the other inns and public houses in the town accounting, no doubt, for the empty streets. The public bar stood still at the approach of strangers; women strangers too. We might well have just stepped off the last London to Aberystwyth stage coach or landed from the moon, but landed there we had and the best was going to be made of it. The fact that I ordered two halves of bitter increased the curiosity of the silent customers, all men, but the landlord obliged with the jollity that befits an ex-matelot. The evidence for this was in the mementos and pictures that covered the walls of his smoke-stained public bar.

The local clientele became less suspicious, more talkative and tentatively helpful when our request for overnight accommodation was made. The landlord explained he had none. Other possibilities were discussed and then rejected on the grounds of cost, unsuitability or too far out of town, and then up spoke a delightful character with a country person's charm; enough to break down all barriers. He offered his wife's service for bed and breakfast, explained how to get there and suggested she was told we had 'met him in chapel'. Another drink, more conversation with the seafaring publican and the first of the many coincidences that were to intrude into my life were to become evident. The innkeeping former sailor had served with one of my brothers in the Royal Navy. Strange as it may seem, this particular coincidence was to be repeated twice over, again with a publican, the future licensee of the 'Duke's Arms' in Broad Street and also the owner of the house I

4

was going to purchase at a later date (although I didn't know it at the time). The three of us had been at the Royal Naval Air Station at Lossiemouth, in the North of Scotland, at the same time and vaguely recalled each other's friends. The landlord to be had been a ship's carpenter, the other an engineering artificer and I was in the Women's Royal Naval Service attached to the Fleet Air Arm. Something should have told me I was destined to visit this seemingly soporific Welsh Border town.

The bridge over the River Lugg is half in Wales, half in England. Stone built hundreds of years ago, it constitutes the borderline between the two countries and its solid structure is etched with the names and messages of love carved into the surface by countless inhabitants and visitors. On the English side is Stapleton House, a Georgian building of ample proportions which served as a guest house and it was there I spent my first night in Presteigne, in a large room at the top of a highly polished staircase that leaned, for no political reason, very much to the left. It only appeared straight after a glass or two of Mrs Davis's home brewed ale.

The overnight stay extended to three days, during which time the first stirrings of a historical adventure drifted through a non-historical mind and I knew that I was about to embark upon a journey that may never have an ending.

At first glance, the town seemed to hide behind a veil of shyness, concealing its medieval past behind Georgian frontages. Patches of cobblestones broke out from under modern day paving slabs, cottage windows of architectural interest invited a closer inspection and tucked in among the houses were part hidden pathways and squares.

The shops, too, did little to encourage passing trade, but why bother, they were a necessity not a tourist attraction. The chemist shop hadn't seen a coat of paint for years, the cycle repair shop often had a lettuce in the window and the old ginger Tom cat slept among the appliances on display at the electrical store. David Fraser's junk shop was a collector's delight, that's if you could find him, and Bill Sid the butcher was perfect for a game of Happy Families. However, it was old Mr Newell's hardware shop that was the essence of the town, a family business established for well over a century; it was a joy to step inside. It still sold oil lamps, candle holders (with or without snuffers), great door locks with large keys, brass knockers, bell pulls and nails made on the nail making machine in the shed at the back. Everything was sold for pounds, shillings and pence and still marked up at the original price. Decimal coinage was not for this shopkeeper, it was real money only.

The three days soon passed, by which time a quiet friendliness towards the strangers blossomed. Pleasantries were passed in shops and inns, casual conversations became more informative and the oddness of this compact little town became even more apparent.

So this was Presteigne, where the curfew bell tolls 105 times each weekday night, at 8.25 pm. A place where life appears slow on the surface but bubbles and boils underneath. Where, for some reason, the scars of past social injustice lie heavily upon the present community. The three day stay was almost at an end when someone mentioned the grave of Mary Morgan; the only grave in the churchyard to have two headstones. Curiosity overtook time and I went for a quick look. It turned out to be the longest look I would ever take.

I stood in the churchyard of St Andrew's, Presteigne and she was all around me. For a fleeting moment it was as if she was reaching out to me to approach her final resting place, to stand and stare at the neat little grave with the two headstones. She wanted me to read the words of the larger one and gasp in disbelief, and hear that gasp carried on the wind that whipped through the overhanging ivy clinging to the old stone wall close by. Then, as if at her request, the setting sun of the autumn evening broke through the lower branches of the ancient elm tree which stood beyond the larger stone and allowed a single shaft of sunlight to illuminate her name, highlighting it from the rest of the words carved upon the smaller gravestone.

I stood alone, with her in my mind. It was as if she was taking me over, pleading with me to resurrect her case and tell the truth, put history straight about what really happened to Mary Morgan.

I sat silently on the grass beside the grave, dallying with my thoughts. What could I do? I wasn't a lawyer, researcher or historian. I was an administrator, a community worker not an academic. What use would I be to her? Yet I knew in the deep corners of my mind it was 'my shout', my turn to face up to my belief that everyone is entitled to a fair hearing, and the fact that she had been dead for over 160 years was no good reason to turn my back on her. That said, I almost would have done had it not been for the fact that I had to pass through the church gate sideways, to allow someone else to enter.

The walk back to reality was a confusing one. I felt I was leaving the scene of a crime, not committed by, but against, a young servant girl and I could not detach myself from the tie she left me with. My knowledge of her crime was negligible, her accusers ghosts in the past and where she came from and who she was, an enigma. All I had was her name, the alleged charge against her and the cold fact that, at the tender age of seventeen, she was hanged by the neck until she was dead. All this, related upon a large, oblong headstone paid for and erected by Thomas Bruce Brudenhal Bruce, Earl of Aylesbury, and the words engraved upon it were the words of Mr Justice George Hardinge, the Judge who passed sentence upon her.

In the short time left before departing westwards, I trawled deeply among the local population, hoping to net a clue or a hint of what had taken place all those years ago but all I got was comment mingled with folklore. The comment expressed the present day feeling with some emotion. The men felt "she must have put 'it about a bit", the women nursed feelings of sadness and shame and a retired past Rector of the town described her as, "A wicked, wicked woman". The flesh was beginning to appear on the skeleton, the gathering folklore padded it out as the locals passed on to me the hand-me-down stories of the myth that surrounded Mary Morgan. Yet despite the chatter, the gossip and what little fact the township offered me, I had the uncanny feeling that somewhere amid the pleasantries and limited co-operation, there was a secret secret, awaiting the upturning of a certain stone or two!

Presteigne, I decided, had written its history upon its gravestones and, having done so, offered it up for examination without fear or favour. In time, I was to be offered some favours plus a few attempts to frighten me off.

My journey continued westwards, through Knighton, the 'Town on the Dyke'. Offa's Dyke is the ancient border of England and Wales, scene of many battles between the two countries. On through Pillith, the battleground on which the Welsh trapped Mortimer's English army and massacred them in the lush valley of the River Lugg, causing the river to flow red through Presteigne and beyond. But still all this was not enough to overtake my thoughts on that young woman in the churchyard at Presteigne, and I knew that one day I would be back to unravel the web of intrigue that surrounded the enigma that was Mary Morgan.

And I did come back. The cottage my friend bought was close to the churchyard, the church tower was clearly visible from the garden and was, I suppose, as close as I could get to Mary Morgan without actually digging in beside her. The high days and holidays spent at Presteigne during the next two years became periods of discovery and I learnt much about the town and its people, past and present, and occasional leaks of information about Mary

Morgan slipped through the subtle wall of silence.

In September 1804  Mary Morgan was brought to Presteigne to spend six months in the County jail, in a town that my historical detective work didn't show up in a good light. Let me take you back there, via its present day setting.

# CHAPTER TWO

## THE PLACE

Presteigne is tucked safely away in the Lugg Valley, just inside the border lands of Mid Wales, a town of ageing architecture, set amid rolling hills and evergreen forests. Its ancient streets, modernised with time, allow the occasional cobblestone to show through, if only to emphasise its historical past. Life in Presteigne, or to give it its Welsh name Llanandras, is slow, never allowing the momentum of living to catch up with it and the town still carries the scars of past battles, which this old county town and its inhabitants have fought with, friend and foe alike.

A compact little place with some 1,450 people living in, or close to, its boundaries it was, until the bureaucratic red tape of government decreed otherwise in 1974, the County town of Radnorshire. For centuries before, it had played host to the Great Sessions of Wales and the Quarter Sessions of the past judicial systems. In its ancient courthouse at the old Shire Hall, were passed the sentences of death on countless offenders incarcerated in the once filthy dungeons below.

Presteigne has changed little since those days and although the shops and advertisements are directed at the consumer needs of the present population, the dress of the day is different and transport has passed from horse to mechanical horsepower, its people will never change. Thus stories and myths are still handed down even today.

Nicknames abound in present day Presteigne recalling past memories; Hard Hat Davis, so called because as the former station master of the now dearly departed change-at-Titley-Junction-for-all-places-west station, he always wore a bowler hat. Fiddler Dick, the watchmaker, would have nine clocks to repair and finish up with ten, but his real claim to fame was his invention of a 'bird scarer' for which he was given a Royal Appointment.

All this adds to the peculiarities of the town. Even the church is conspicuous by its oddness: St Andrew's church, a Scottish name, within the English diocese of Hereford and standing on Welsh soil.

Every weekday night, at 8.25 pm, the curfew is rung from the old church tower. The tenor bell breaking into the silence of the evening takes you back to 1565, when John Beddoes founded the grammar school, linking its endowment to the daily ringing. The rent from a field a mile to the west of the town, known as Bell Meadow, provided the payment for the bell ringer.

Presteigne past was a town of custom, pomp, pageantry and celebration. The customs were many and included the annual fairs, most of which took place on the 'Warden', the open space above the town, the site on which Presteigne Castle once stood during the days of the Lord Marchers and beyond. It is even believed to have been a British outpost, watching over the River Lugg before the Mercian advances of the eighth and ninth centuries. The Warden site is thought to have been presented as a gift to the town in 1805 by the Fifth Earl of Oxford, but his daughter Lady Langdale challenged this about seventy years later, when written evidence could not be found to prove it. Records do establish, however, that the Warden was used long before this as an open public area. The pleasure fair was held on the Warden for many years and was known as the 'Warden Wake'. The number of fairs held in the town annually varied over the ages, but was always in the region of five or six.

The town also had its market days, given under charter in 1482 by Richard Martin, the Bishop of St David's, a native of Presteigne. Market day was Saturday and remained so until 1841, but during this time it lost its popularity to Kington and Knighton, although the opening of the new market hall in 1865 saw a revival in its fortunes and the day was again changed to a Wednesday. There is no present day market.

Causes for celebration were many and took the form of balls and entertainments, but until the opening of the assembly rooms over the market hall, Presteigne events took place out of town in neighbouring halls. Once accommodation in the town became available, gatherings became very fashionable and were known as County Balls; these were succeeded in the late 1800s by the Hunt Balls.

The Victorian era brought endless dances, organised by the Friendly Societies and Agricultural Associations of the town. There were, of course, private functions held in the great houses throughout the district, but whatever the occasion they never ended before the dawn.

Causes for general celebration were produced at the slightest whim. Coming of age parties, newlyweds returning from honeymoon, births and christenings, even the passing of popular Acts of Parliament prompted the organisation of public celebration. Dinners and tea parties on Royal occasions, paid for by public subscription, were enjoyed by all classes of the community and remain so to this day.

Entertainment was usually provided by strolling players. John Ward's Company spent a month in Presteigne in the summer of 1758. His grand-daughter, Sarah Siddons, is said to have performed with the Company at that time, but as she was only a child of three this seems unlikely. The last visit to Presteigne by a dramatic company was by Mr Waldergraves' Company of Theatrical Players in 1818. The town has always relied on its own talents since then and has continued to do so, on and off, through the years.

Pomp and pageantry arrived with the coming of the judiciary. It was decreed in 1542 that the Great Sessions of Wales should be held alternately with New Radnor, but after the Civil War it was held only in the County town and for well over three hundred years the visit of the English Judge, twice a year, was an event to cause a public stir. Until the end of the eighteenth century, the roads were unsuitable for carriages so the judge and his procession of barristers, law officers and servants entered the town on horseback. He would be met about a mile out of town by the High Sheriff and other dignitaries, with trumpeters and pikemen in attendance. It was a grand spectacle which became even more impressive with the introduction of coaches during the late 1700s. There was always a splendid luncheon, followed by a service at the Parish Church, before the court opened its session.

Old customs maintained their popularity for many years. The maypole in the market square, the curfew, the burning of the bush over the wheatfields on New Year's morning and keeping a loaf, specially baked on Good Friday, would ward off evil for the rest of the year. Many people hung branches of the Mountain Ash tree over their doors on May Day, in the hope of keeping witches and fairies at bay.

An important position in the community was that of town crier, and equal rights to the post were introduced as early as 1839 when a woman was appointed to the position.

Industry was chiefly farming, although malting was an important trade up to the nineteenth century. Tanning was another source of employment during the Victorian age, succeeded by saw milling, and there was also the weaving business of John Beddoes, the founder of the Grammar School, who endowed the curfew ringing.

Social development was slow. At the turn of the twentieth century, there was no electricity, telephone or proper water supply. The railway was well established, so was the telegraph system and gas supplies to households able to afford it. Gas was also available for streetlighting, but until then houses and shops were lit by candle and rush light, including public buildings like the Shire Hall and the Assembly Rooms.

Motor cars were unknown until the early Edwardian era and when they did arrive the council imposed a speed restriction of six miles per hour, in the hope that they could 'combat the menace on the roads'. Road safety was uppermost in Presteigne it seems, as only three years previous to the introduction of the motor car, a pedal cyclist had been found guilty of 'furious driving' and was fined ten shillings, with seven and six pence costs.

In those days the people of Presteigne liked a drink - and still do! Records show that from the middle of the eighteenth century, there were twenty-nine inns or hostelries in the town. By the turn of the twentieth century this had been reduced to fourteen and in present day Presteigne there are seven. Most of the old inns still stand today as private dwelling houses.

It is, however, at the place of the dead that I start my historical meanderings, through a town that is more white than black and white, that spills across the English border having scant regard for territorial rights, where you die in Wales and are buried in England; a schizophrenic journey on the way to their Mecca.

The Parish Church of St Andrew, approached through the Scallions, overlooked by Church View cottages and Oak Villas and adjoined by the walled garden of the Old Rectory, stands resplendent, proudly revealing its ancient architectural beauty to all and sundry. The grey stone memorials to the dead stand in uneven rows, some propped up beside the old stone wall that hides the rectory garden from the curious eye of the casual visitor. These are the gravestones of the past, cut and scored and weathered with time, the patiently carved letters and words part hidden under clusters of mossy patches. All that is needed to invite enquiry is a little sign that reads, "lift the moss to expose history".

A short distance from the main church entrance are the two stones that mark one grave. The large one, potent in its arrogance, states in etched lettering upon the flaking background:

"To the memory of Mary Morgan who young and beautiful, endowed with a good understanding and disposition but unenlightened by the sacred truths of christianity, became the victim of sin and shame and was condemned to an ignominious death on the 11th April 1805 for the murder of her bastard Child. Roused to a first sense of guilt and remorse by the eloquent and humane exertions of her benevolent judge Mr Justice Hardinge, she underwent the sentence of the law on the following Thursday with unfeigned repentance and a fervent hope of forgiveness through the merits of a redeeming intercessor. This stone is erected not merely to perpetuate the remembrance of a departed penitent, but to remind the living of the frailty of human nature when unsupported by religion."

Once more I stared at the stone, once more I felt her presence urging me to go on. I brushed away the moss and pulled up the long grass hiding the inscription at the bottom of the stone and there it clearly stated "Thomas Bruce Brudenell Bruce, Earl of Aylesbury".

I already knew that the words were those of the Judge but what had it got to do with Lord Aylesbury?

The gravestone established, rightly or not, that Mary had murdered her bastard child, a common enough crime at the time. Could Lord

Aylesbury be a contender for "Father of the murdered child"? Too simple to contemplate, better to rule him out now. Perhaps he was just a kindly gentleman, a social reformer, even a rich benefactor of the Judge. Nothing quite so interesting turned up in the researches. The association between Hardinge and Aylesbury was not clearly defined, except that they were both members of Parliament serving areas of Wiltshire, but I noted in my mind that, at some point, I had better have a good look at the Judge's antecedence, although I hadn't any idea of where to make a start.

The comment upon the fate of Mary Morgan, written upon her gravestone, angered me but the smaller one smoothed me out again. Gentle in comparison but never overshadowed, even at sunset, by the larger stone, it was erected by the townspeople of the day and their simple message conveyed all to the reader. Quite obviously upset by the heartlessness of a judge who could condemn so short a life to such a cruel end, the people of Presteigne, normally split by the class structure, shared their grief with each other and had these words engraved upon the stone.

"In memory of Mary Morgan who suffered
April 13th 1805 aged seventeen years
He that is without sin among you
Let him first cast the stone at her
The 18th chapter of St John
part of the 7th verse."

I can understand the need for the stone but the message held more than met the eye. Somewhere in that biblical tract was hidden the secret secret of Presteigne.

The quietness of the present day township seemed to haunt me. It was as if it was feeling guilty about its past and it bugged me. It was time I went back into history to stroll through the town during Mary Morgan's time and let her be my guide.

It was obvious that the town was not the quiet place it is today. Poverty was rife, the class sytem at its height and crime prevailed at all levels. Young girls were taken, at the early age of twelve and thirteen, into the service of the upper classes where they were used and abused by the males of the household. Orders of bastardy were prolific in the town and the courts were constantly in use. Drunkenness was habitual and there was no police force to keep law and order. Pikemen, or javelinmen as they were known, were the only obvious signs of policing, but they had no real effect on the prevention of crime or on social conditions.

The coming of the nineteenth century produced the years of progress in trade and transport throughout England and Wales. Napoleon was at war with Britain, young men were being called in to serve with the armies and medical experiments were publicly made on the bodies of those hanged for crimes.

Despite the gloom of war and poverty, the fashions of the day were bright and colourful blues, purple, geranium red and rose pink. Dresses were low cut, with plain sleeves, decorated with lace inserts and tucks drawn around the bosom. But these were not for the likes of Mary Morgan and her kind. These clothes were worn by the rich of Presteigne and the surrounding areas.

As the County town, Presteigne was the hub of rural life. The Justices of the Peace often met in the best inn parlours to discuss pressing problems of the poor, matters of indiscipline and the raising of taxes, as well as generally gossiping and doing business. Travel was almost entirely on horseback, the roads an unending procession of pack horse and riders with strings of additional horses in tow, the lead horse wearing bells. There were also pedestrian cattle herds, flocks of sheep with gangs of drovers, parties of soldiers and itinerant tradesmen. Wheeled vehicles were scarce and were only owned by the very wealthy. It was the custom for the average farmer to mount his horse on the stone mounting block in his own yard and for his wife to take her seat behind him, pillion style. The roads were little better than dirt tracks, rutted, dry and dusty in the summer, muddy in the winter. The ditches were often filled with stinking water and sewage, so powerful persons like Members of Parliament, county officials and magistrates usually arranged for the county surveyor to ensure that the best roads were conveniently sited close to their houses.

The turnpikes were coming into existence at this time, but these were toll roads and nobody liked paying tolls, particularly as the toll collectors often used their position to extract more money than was due. The main turpike road to Aberystwyth was opened in about 1750 and Presteigne became a coaching stopover, where the inns and hostelries were constantly habited by strangers.

The working classes made their own soap at home, by burning green ferns and rolling the ashes into balls. The average worker regarded butcher's meat as a real luxury; he usually relied on his own animals or sharing with others. Tea was the beverage of the rich; cider and water sufficed for the ordinary folk.

Wages varied; pantrymaids earned from £4 4s to £5 5s per annum, undermaids £2 to £2 50s per annum and dairymaids £3 to £4 4s per annum.

Cock fighting was a popular Presteigne sport and pastime and often took place on the north side of the churchyard, the side not used for burying the dead. This was known locally as the devil's side. Before a fight, the trainer got the bird into condition on a diet of sweet butter, white sugar candy and finely chopped Rosemary, mixed with wheatmeal, oatmeal and the white of an egg. This staple diet for fighting cocks was far above the standard of food the poor and suffering enjoyed and highlighted the substantial gap between rich and poor.

The churchyard was also the location for funerals and, until the Methodist revival, they were occasions for drunkeness, feasting and jollity, when poverty and wretchedness were forgotten. Warm beer was always a favourite at these times.

Public whipping was a common punishment and it was not rare to see a woman stripped to the waist and whipped by the jailer or his deputy. Her body would be beaten whilst on route from the jail door to the Town Hall and back again and then she would be discharged. Women suffered this punishment to their backs until 1817, usually for the 'crime' of adultery. There is no record of a man being punished for

this crime, although they were whipped for
other forms of crime. The last man to be
whipped in Presteigne was in 1828.

Into this town, during the autumn of
1804, came a sixteen year old servant girl to
be incarcerated in the filthy, rat infested
cell to answer to a charge of murder.

I stood on the steps of the Shire Hall and
took it all in, breathed the foul air of the
past, imagined the cock fighting and the bull
baiting taking place across the road from
where I was standing and wondered whether some
people, even today, burnt the bush or hung the
mountain ash branch over the front door to
ward off present day witches and fairies. No
wonder it bugged me!

On my next visit to Presteigne six months
later, I stood on the same steps and rang the
brass bell on the front door of the Shire
Hall. The custodian had agreed to show me
around the court room and the dungeons. I had
been back to the graveside to communicate with
my obsession, for that is what it had become,
and felt that I needed to see for myself the
place in which they had imprisoned the young
girl I had allowed to encroach upon my life.
Since I had last been to the town, I had
travelled 24,000 miles, a round trip to New
Zealand, and still I couldn't blot out Mary
Morgan. Out of sight, out of mind meant
nothing to me. I had spent six months
adjusting to the Antipodean end of my family,
getting to know nephews and nieces I had never
met and exploring a beautiful country. Some
parts of that landscape were so uncannily like
Mid Wales that I was constantly reminded of a
Welsh Border Town and a case of legal murder

that I was determined to bring to moral if not lawful justice.

On my return to England I settled into new employment, directing community services. I was enjoying a political awareness in my life and expanding my contribution to the cause of women's rights. Despite all this, my ordered way of life was occasionally nudged into disorder after casual visits to that black and white township that I had not yet come to terms with. I wondered if I ever would.

It was autumn 1975 when I stood on the steps of the Shire Hall, rang the bell and awaited the caretaker. She was friendly, although a little distant, and immediately set about her particular tour of the premises with her special line of patter. Mary Morgan, it seemed, was a servant girl at Newcastle Court, a large country house just outside Presteigne, when she found herself pregnant. The father of the child was thought to be a member of the gentry who would not take responsibility for Mary or her child. Common place in those days, an ordinary incident, an ordinary story. What was I getting so obsessive about? A quick look round the Shire Hall and I would call it a day.

Not so! At the end of the mini tour, the caretaker casually threw in, "They did say that the father of the child was on the jury that found her guilty". What! No jury vetting in those days. Could that really be true?

I felt Mary's presence telling me it was. She was there with me as I stood in the dock, with me as I sat in the cell, with me as I walked to Gallows Lane and sat on the stump of the tree from which she had hung in 1805.

23

It isn't the same court now, although very similar, but I believe the cell is the same one. I sat in it all alone and thought about Mary as she shared the darkness and I wondered what kind of legal system allowed a young girl to be tried for the murder of her child and the suspected father of that child to sit among the twelve just men and true who were eventually to find her guilty. It could only be corrupt, class structured and biased. Or was I? You must be my judge.

# CHAPTER THREE

## THE LEGAL SYSTEM


In 1805 the organisation of the judiciary was not clear, with no real difference between barristers and judges, so that there was little professional rivalry existing between them. There were many honorary posts with salaries paid to a nominee, while the subordinates did the work. Payment was by fee and this gave the bench an opportunity to prolong proceedings. Judges were appointed by the King through the Lord Chancellor and his nominations usually favoured the political party in office (Whigs or Tories). The Lord Chancellor was a Cabinet Minister.

In about 1800 attorneys, who were the local lawyers as opposed to the barristers who came from the London Inns of Court, began to be known as solicitors. This was potentially a very good job by which to become wealthy and influential.

Landlords would often put matters of land and property management into their hands, employing them as a clerk. In this capacity they became involved with the local power base and could assist the land owner in legal matters, although the landlord, usually a magistrate, had great power. The bar was a place of class distinction and snobbery and the four Inns of Court at the City of London gates were the practising ground for their business. The wealthiest barristers spent the season at Bath enjoying the circuits and they usually followed the Westminster judges into the provinces on their regular round of the

Assizes. By doing this, they brought the fashionable living styles of London and Bath with them.

Judges were, as a rule, not permitted to sit in the Commons, although it seems that those serving Wales were exempt from this. Nomination to the bench was, in most cases, the choice of the membership of the House of Commons.

Trials were strange affairs, where the practice of the law was such that each trial was almost a professional conference between the judges and the barristers on either side, all of whom were usually members of the same body, usually trained in the same school and differing only in their rank in the legal hierarchy. The objectives of these meetings was to discover how the past decisions of the court could be applied to the present case. The only paid judges were those from Westminster, the only barristers were those from London. There was no police force as such in existence, although volunteer bands of locals were often organised to patrol the streets at night particularly if crime was on the increase.

The judges went to the people, usually on circuit, once a year in the four northern counties and twice a year elsewhere but they did not stay long. Meanwhile the County was required to make its own provision for law and order, allowing local officials to become powerful. In England and Wales, Central Government did little to secure public safety, provide schools, repair roads or offer relief to the poor. With the exception of the postal service, the State performed very little to benefit the tax payer.

The representatives of Central Government, like customs officers, treasury and tax men, excise agents and postal officials were very unpopular, without any social standing and low paid. Of all these the excise agents were the most disliked; it was they who collected the duty on alcoholic beverages. These officials had inquisitorial powers, supported by the law, and had total authority to tax the people. As collectors of direct taxes, a power granted to them by the local aristocracy, they had become a symbol of arbitrary government.

The real power in the land was held by the landlords, the local landowners; these were the real rulers of the provinces. From among this body were chosen, according to long established custom, the main group of Justices of the Peace. These magistrates met at regular intervals and their meetings were of three kinds: Special Sessions, Petty Sessions and Quarter Sessions. The Quarter Sessions were held every three months and all magistrates were required to attend. No real legal knowledge was required of them and they usually judged by common sense, or at least were expected to do so. For most petty offences they would sit alone or in pairs to judge and pass sentence, otherwise cases were referred to the Quarter Sessions. The magistrates also performed administrative as well as judicial functions. They could summon the people of the Parish and require them to pay for the repair of a local road or building that had fallen into disrepair and the parishioners were compelled to meet the cost. In this capacity they also approved the Parish Rate for the upkeep of the roads, the Poor

Rate and they fixed the amount of the County Rate. They were generally responsible to the crown for the administration of the Parishes and the Hundreds and they appointed, in each Parish, a constable to work for them in policing the district. They also had a surveyor of highways and an overseer to administer the Poor Law.

Magistrates had to be resident in the County and own, in their County, land which provided them with a net income of at least one hundred pounds, thus guaranteeing the continuation of the aristrocratic nature of the institution.

The selection of magistrates had been established throughout the century and were chosen on the recommendation of the Lord Lieutenant of the County; this office being customarily given to the largest landowner in the County. Although they were technically answerable to the crown, the Justices of the Peace relied upon the local aristocracy for appointment and promotion. It was therefore possible to be admitted to the ranks of JP simply by purchasing land or performing various 'special' duties for the High Sheriff, an honour coveted by all the 'nouveau riche' of the neighbourhood.

It was a system which was anything but democratic. The JP was an aristocrat who, without jury or any regular procedure, decided upon a collection of matters, often largely affecting his own property. Generally, their administration of justice does appear to have been easy going and kindly. This kindliness though was not altogether remarkable, for the JPs not only lacked the will to oppress the public but had no means of control. The magistrates had no organised forces to call upon to check the growth of crime and they had to rely upon Parliament to tighten the penal code.

It is shocking that in 1800, over two hundred offences were capital. The few measures of policing available at this time included the establishment of soldiers in barracks in the country districts, but generally England and Wales was governed without a police service. The local organisations supported this system with the church wardens, constables, highway surveyors and the overseers of the poor very heavily involved in the administration of the policing.

The Royal Radnorshire Militia had their Headquarters at Presteigne for over two hundred years, and they were often called upon to maintain law and order. The barracks were at Garrison House in Church Street.

The method of choosing jurors was strange. The law stated that twelve jurors should be chosen by lot from a list, made up for each session of the Assizes, containing anything from forty-eight to seventy-two names. Enormous rights of challenge were granted to the contending parties but once constituted, the twelve jurors heard the speeches of counsel, the evidence and the Judge's summing up. After this they retired into an adjoining room where, in order to avoid delaying the proceedings, they were kept without food, drink, heat or light unless the permission of the Judge was given. They were left like that until they were all unanimously agreed upon a verdict. This, in particular, referred to civil cases.

In criminal cases, the law required that before a jury of twelve were elected to try a case, a grand jury of twenty-four members had to examine the case beforehand and refer it to trial. As a further precaution, the coroner would enquire into all cases of violent and sudden death, but only as the president of the jury. Jurors were only required to determine the question of fact; it was up to the Judge or the professional magistrate to determine the question of the law. As the line between fact and law was not always very clear, a clever Judge, in his summing up, could put the question of fact before the jurors in a language so skilful and manipulating that he left the jury no real share in the final decision. On the other hand, an indolent Judge could blurr the picture to such an extent, that argument between the Crown and the press on this matter was constant for the fifty years up to 1800.

The scene at the time of the court taking place was incredible. The Circuit Judge would arrive from Westminster in great style, giving cause for countless festivities to begin throughout the whole County and were often described as an afternoon's diversion. The Judge took his position at his bench looking rather like the father in the midst of his family, his appearance was unthreatening and, according to ancient custom, flowers were thrown upon his desk and upon that of the clerk. It is extraordinary that the Judge permitted his bench to be invaded by throngs of spectators and was often surrounded by the prettiest of the women of the County. These were usually the sisters or wives of the Grand Jury and dressed in the most elegant style. It was a common enough sight to see the Judge's venerable head overloaded with a large wig, peering out among the adoring female faces. Ladies would put on their best bonnets in the morning just to look at the Judge and to hear him condemn his prisoners to death. When the trial was over, they would leave to prepare for the dancing at the Assize Ball that evening, an important event in the social calendar of the gentry. The Judge's presence always created an enormous stir throughout the entire community and it must have been an impressive sight to see the gathering of barristers, clerks and soldiers which accompanied the judicial train.

Stealing goods to the value of five shillings or more or picking pockets were among the two hundred crimes which attracted the death penalty. An assault upon the person usually meant a fine of a shilling and there was quite a degree of leniency in dealing with the assault because the more senior the person assaulted, the heavier the fine. Transportation became a common punishment for offenders against the law and magistrates had powers to inflict a sentence of penal servitude for trivial crimes, like the one passed upon a young girl who was sent to the colonies for seven years for stealing linen from a washing line.

The Presteigne Sessions in those days were anything but quiet, and there are records of people in the streets being disciplined for causing breaches of the peace by letting off fireworks and shouting obscenities.

The jail itself is another matter. Its dark, filthy dungeons lay beneath the courtroom in sole charge of a jailer. Sexes were not segregated and female prisoners were looked after by the male jailer. Prisoners received one pound of bread per day and had no blankets, sleeping only on straw. The prisoners themselves deteriorated in the filthy conditions. Each prison had a tap, under the supervision of the jailer, and ale was served to those who could afford it. This was known as the tap system. Strangely enough, prisoners were expected to pay the cost of their conveyance to the jail, though usually they had no money to make this payment. The jailer's annual salary was only twenty pounds and, needless to say, he would seek other ways of gaining extra payment from the prisoners, the selling of ale being a common practice.

A prison chaplain, usually the Rector, was also appointed and he received a fee of fifteen pounds a year, for which he was required to attend the condemned prisoners every Sunday, on festival days and every day during Passion week. Despite their Christian attitudes, this was not always carried out and there is a report which states that in 1818 two prisoners in the jail, under sentence of death, reported to the Court that they had not been visited by the chaplain, despite the fact that the jail was almost opposite his house. The Rector also received two guineas for attending criminals at their execution and seven shillings and sixpence for printing their confessions.

Such was the undisciplined attitude of the Court at that time, that should the weather be cold or conditions in the courthouse not suited to the visiting Judge or his retinue, the Court would be closed and re-opened an hour or so later in the main bar of the nearest inn; thus ensuring a greater degree of comfort, combined with good food and drink.

Court day was always Fair day in Presteigne. The town filled up with people, and an atmosphere of fun, amusement, jollity and companionship prevailed. A variety of public entertainments on the day included boxing, cock fighting, bull baiting and dog prailling. Boxing was a brutal affair, the competitors having the right to strangle their opponent and also to beat him to death with iron rimmed clogs. Bear and bull baiting consisted of tying the animal to a post and allowing it to be worried by a pack of dogs. Often the dogs would be called off, allowing time for the fight to be continued over several days before the huge beast was finally killed. Prailling dogs involved fastening a dog's tail to a bullock's horn and letting them loose. The crowd would then follow the beasts to observe the fun.

It would be fair to say that interest in these bloody sports was carried over to the hangings and Presteigne on hanging day was a scene of great excitement and anticipation. It was these conditions and events which caused William Wilberforce to write, "The barbarous custom of hanging has been tried too long and with a success which might have been expected from it. The most effective way of preventing greater crimes is by punishing the smaller and endeavouring to repress the general spirit of licentiousness, which is the parent of every species of vice". Wilberforce also had high hopes that a more severe public morality would render the criminal code unnecessary.

A great friend of Wilberforce, Sir Samuel Romilly, who had associations at Knill Court, close to Presteigne, was a great, social reformer of the day and in his capacity as Solicitor General and a Member of Parliament he reduced substantially the numbers of crimes subjected to a hanging decision.

Prisoners tried before these Courts could say little, if anything, in their defence and it must have been an awesome moment for those brought before the judiciary.

Before the Great Sessions held in Presteigne during the month of April 1805, Mary Morgan, then just seventeen years old, was brought before the Court to be tried by a Judge and jury acting within the confines of an undisciplined court, unable to say anything in her own defence, to be tried by a decadent and favoured judicial system.

Well, was I right, was it a bad system? It does appear to be riddled with class discrimination and favouritism. No farm labourers or those in service allowed to sit on a jury. The working class could not be tried by their peers, so what chance did they have of an acquittal? Perhaps a dog's chance - if you could afford a defence counsel.

But where was all this background information getting me? I was in a historical maze and couldn't get out. Every turn was blocked by myth and legend, distortion, hearsay and closed doors. Yet all through my basic examination of a town and its past, there was a constant, nagging voice that said, "Go for it". So I did.

# CHAPTER FOUR

## THE MOMENTUM

By the middle of 1976 Mary Morgan had become so involved with my life she had become a major part of it and a decision had to be made. I either had to drop her altogether or give her all I had got. I chose the latter and moved to Presteigne.

Emotionally, it was a very difficult time. My mother was getting older and would obviously miss me being close at hand and I had other attachments and involvements that were hard to dissolve. I would have to free myself from my commitments to the feminist movement, although I had no difficulty in convincing myself that, as a good feminist, Mary Morgan had need of my commitment also. Despite all this personal pressure, her call on my time was greater now than it had ever been.

I sold my house, gave up my job and with no prospects of employment I prepared for the move West. My friend had agreed to come as well. She had found employment as a part time social worker in a town nearby and this would provide a basic income for us. Nevertheless, I felt it was important to have a place of my own, so I purchased a little eighteenth century house on the High Street, a house that Mary passed by on her way to the gallows. The property was an investment for my capital, a place to accumulate my possesions and thoughts, a bolt hole to hide in if things got rough.

How to earn a living was the all important question and as the date for the move drew near, I became more anxious about my future. I moved on 23 September 1976, 171 years to the day on which Mary Morgan killed her child, yet another coincidence on the way to my story.

The removal van arrived, my mother cried and off I went in my MG Midget with the Tabby cat tranquilised in the back and my friend in her car with the Ginger cat well sedated too. It was the same route as that very first journey five years before. Mortimers Cross, Shobdon, The Bell at Byton and there was Presteigne, partially visible through the early autumn mist, but this time I was not the casual visitor, this time I was coming to stay. No turning back, no regrets . . . yet. The van was unloaded, personal effects distributed between the two premises but as Garden Cottage was already furnished from its days as a holiday retreat, it was comfortable from the start.

It was strange to think that I was now 'at home' in Presteigne and I was looking forward to becoming part of the community. Mary Morgan was uppermost in my thoughts now and it would have been so easy to have leaned into the Presteigne way of life and 'got by' somehow, without having to work. However, I had to be practical and find a way of earning a living before my savings ran out. In the end, I decided the best thing was to work for myself so I converted my house into a coffee shop, selling wholefoods on the side.

My house became 'The Happy Nut and The Coffee Pot' and whether the local population, plus the summer tourists, would make it a

36

viable proposition was anybody's guess, but I was prepared to give it three years. Meanwhile it gave me the freedom to research my story and I set about gleaning information day by day. Old and new friends were helpful, kind and practical and I valued their help and support.

'The Coffee Pot' became a regular meeting place for the locals and, in accordance with the Presteigne custom, I was given a nickname and referred to as the "Happy Nut at the Coffee Pot'. It was from this place that many local activities had their beginnings, because I believed that to move into a new community meant giving something back to it, if only to compensate for the benefits it was giving me.

The Presteigne Entertainers took the stage at Christmas with a pantomime which I wrote and directed and, for the next three or four years, productions and shows of all types were to become part of the social scene, which then went on tour to other nearby villages. The Presteigne Museum established its beginnings over a few cups of coffee and now flourishes in the old servants' quarters at the Shire Hall and other local activities stemmed from similar meetings. Regular gatherings discussed politics, world affairs and day to day events and the 'Coffee Pot' became a popular part of community life. It was personally pleasing to hear it referred to as "The Left Bank of Presteigne".

The little cafe on the High Street became a way of life for me with its regular groupies like 'Derek the Hairdresser', 'Liz the Cakemaker', 'Godfrey the Chemist', 'David the Antique Dealer', 'Charlie the Copper', 'Des the Traffic Warden' (once monthly), 'Stan the

Runner', 'Eddie Mac' and dear 'Lord Nicholas'. They were all principals in the social tapestry of present day Presteigne, their collective good humour keeping me going through the bad moments and their hints of local history opening up the road to Mary Morgan's beginnings.

A highlight of that first autumn in Presteigne was when I was asked to be Guest of Honour at the Cricket Club annual dinner. I had to 'swot up' very quickly, on the cricketing heroes of Presteigne and I managed to produce a humorous after dinner speech, which I feel convinced them I wasn't too bad with a bat and ball myself in my day. It was a rumbustious evening, one of the modern day celebrations that didn't end until dawn.

The first stop on the road to Mary Morgan was Aberystwyth, site of the National Library of Wales. I went off for the day with Bryn, a good friend from my community work days, who had become taken up with my obsession and, in those early days of long laborious research, he gave me a great deal of help. We spent many days entombed in the depths of the manuscripts department, totally absorbed in the annals of Welsh legal history, pouring over the records of the Great Sessions of Wales and going off at a tangent only to find similar cases. And then we found them and touched them; the handwritten recordings of the trial of Mary Morgan. They were dusty, dirty and nibbled at the edges by rats, but that didn't matter. In the midst of the august company of fellow researchers, Bryn and I shared a hug, made a few notes and went for a celebratory pint.

The game was on, the rules laid down and I
was under starter's orders for a challenge
match that was going to be all consuming.
Somewhere along the way I lost Bryn to Saudi
Arabia, just as I was to lose other close
friends and lovers for differing reasons but I
knew my destiny was tied up with that of Mary
Morgan as I set out to lay her ghost and put
the record straight on her behalf, if I could.

But who was she? The trial records gave
little away, except to say that she was a
servant to Walter Wilkins Esquire of
Maesllwych, but the newspapers gave away a
little bit more.

The Cambrian on Saturday 6 October 1804
reported that, "Last week, a female servant
who lived in the house of a most respectable
gentleman in Radnorshire was committed to the
County jail for the murdur of her new born
child". A simple press statement that linked
a place called Maesllwych with a sixteen year
old servant girl and a "respectable"
Radnorshire gentleman.

I paused to collect my thoughts and collate
my notes. Who, what, where was Maesllwych?
Why had W H Howse, the noted Radnorshire
historian and writer, in his recordings of the
incident placed the girl and her crime at
Newcastle Court? Why would he deliberately
mislead? It was all very odd. I had to
locate Maesllwych, but no-one could or would
help me, most likely because I could not
pronounce its Welsh name properly.

I was at a loss as to what to do next. It
was suggested by an anonymous adviser that I
read 'A Welsh Border Town' by W H Howse, to
see if that would help but I wasn't too
hopeful, bearing in mind his error over siting

the killing. Anyway, I couldn't get hold of a copy at short notice.

A week or two later, I was in the loft at home, looking for a packing case lost in the move, when I noticed a loose slate had allowed a single shaft of sunlight into the roof space. It alighted upon what looked like a small package, tucked under the eaves. I carefully trod across the ceiling joists and made my way towards the end of the sunlight. To my amazement, it wasn't a package but a perfectly good copy of the Howse book I had not been able to get hold of and it was signed by the author too. Yet another coincidence? Who knows. It didn't clear up the Wilkins' connection but it gave me some good background material.

I was running out of road when something or someone intervened and opened it up again. It was on the way to visit a close friend who lived in Brecon that I had to stop for the lavatory, so I pulled into the village of Glasbury-on-Wye. I called at the local inn and was stunned to find it was the 'Maesllwych Arms'. I decided to stay and ask a few questions about the Wilkins' family home. Silence, cold stoney silence, broken only by an old gentleman who, on the strength of a large scotch, told me to seek out a local woman who was writing a history of Glasbury. He did, however, also caution me with the words, "If I was you missus, I would'na meddle".

Meddle I was going to, come hell or high water. I found out that the castle on the hillside, overlooking the River Wye, was Maesllwych, owned by a Major De Winton who, I later discovered, was the direct descendent of

40

Walter Wilkins the First, employer of Mary Morgan. The jigsaw puzzle was coming together, but without the help of the De Wintons and the local inhabitants of Glasbury and I knew why! When I asked the local historian why she thought W H Howse had sited the crime elsewhere, all she said was, "Warned off my dear, I expect". Warned off was he? Well, no-one was warning me off. Anyway, what had "a most respectable gentleman living in Radnorshire" in 1804 got to hide.

Burke's Peerage and Landed Gentry here I come, plus any other books of reference that might give me an insight into "a respectable gentleman" called Walter Wilkins.

# CHAPTER FIVE

## THE WILKINS

The harsh winter of 1977-78 stopped me in my tracks. It brought everyone and everything in Presteigne to a virtual standstill. The snow fell almost continually for weeks on end and the snow ploughs worked hard to keep the town open but, despite the efforts of the County Highways Department, Presteigne, along with many other small towns and villages, was cut off and almost isolated. It was difficult to manoeuvre the pavements on foot, let alone the roadways by car. Supplies were running low and I was feeling frustrated at my lack of communication with the outside world of research, books and documents as well as my family and friends.

The town kept cheerful throughout the ice age grip winter had on it and an enormous amount of goodwill radiated from all around. Mary's grave was lost beneath great, sweeping waves of whiteness which lay unbroken for months but we still kept in touch, although my visits to her grave were few and far between. I did stagger to it one Sunday morning, hopeful that the Churchgoers had beaten a path across the churchyard. They had and somehow I made it to the grave guided, of course, by her presence.

It proved to be a fruitful journey because on the way home I met the Librarian, who told me that she thought the library van would get through that week with the new supplies of books, including my requests. They came in due course and I was back into it again. The winter seemed mundane as I mulled over the antecedence of a certain Walter Wilkins.

The country gentleman's house in Wales at the turn of the eighteenth century was entirely self-supporting. Wine was one of the very few items bought in, usually in barrels from Bristol. Home made beer was the main drink and the footman, as well as accepting his usual duties, was required to act as brewmaster.

The lady of the house would provide medicines extracted from various herbs that lay to hand. Meadow Saffron blended with brandy made a wine good for gout, Speedwell was good for easing haemorrhoids, Broom Seeds mixed into hot ale, and taken every morning, provided a remedy for the stones and a good cough mixture could be made by boiling Liverpool ale with Rosemary, honey and salt butter. One important member of the household was usually the laundry maid, whose duties were to ensure that the elaborate caps and headresses for her mistress, as well as the plainer caps for the serving maids, were always crisp, clean and ready for use.

The most cheerful room in the house was the kitchen where there was a large fire, plenty of food and good company. Casual visitors included the tailor, weaver, cobbler, packmen and other trades people, who came to deliver orders and enjoy the warm hospitality. Outside, servants would gather and sit at mealtimes with the rest of the staff and partake in the idle gossip which was always available, with the cook or housekeeper leading or controlling the chatter depending on its content. Cooking was carried out in enormous iron pots suspended over the huge fire. In the intense heat the great room below stairs was constantly filled by the aroma of good food. At Christmas time, local carol singers would call to entertain the family and their guests, later returning to the hospitality of the kitchen and enjoying ale, good food and company provided with seasonal goodwill by the household. Guests of the family stayed for months, so the kitchens were always kept busy and the volume of work was high. Servants were on call twenty-four hours a day in case a late supper or an early breakfast was needed; the servants either staying up till ordered to bed or rising sufficiently early to get the fires lit for the cooking.

It was a grand way of life for the gentry, waited upon hand and foot, consuming the finest of provisions and attended to by faithful servants, beholden to their employers for their only source of income.

Walter Wilkins was the owner of such a fine house. The second son of John Wilkins of The Priory, Brecon, he was born on 15 November 1741, and was educated at Christ College, Brecon before being placed on the foundation of Winchester College. From there, he progressed to the London Academy and obtained, through the connections of his mother who was related to the Lord Chancellor, Lord Camden, a nomination to the Indian Civil Service.

He arrived in India at an early age and in those formative years he became connected with Robert Clive, later to be Lord Clive, who at that time was a company clerk to a Colonel in the Indian Army. (Clive eventually became the ruler of Bengal.) In comparison with Wilkins' success, Robert Clive returned to England in

1760 and became the MP for Shrewsbury, maintaining the seat until his death, by suicide, in 1774. (He cut his throat.)

Wilkins soon established himself in India, and immediately set about obtaining his promotions, eventually becoming the first Governor of the Province of Chittygong. This was followed by an appointment to the Supreme Council of Bengal, a state administered by the Nawab but whose military power lay in the hands of the East India Company who used it to help themselves and to give their merchants a free run of the country's internal trade. Any merchant able to hire a few followers could browbeat the Nawabi officers and intimidate the villagers to their own advantage, and the sponsored State of Bengal soon became known as 'The Plundered State of Bengal'. It was financially bled white. Between 1769 and 1770, the final years of Wilkins stay in the East India Company and in the Indian Civil Service, famine killed over one million people, although Robert Walpole stated that this figure was nearer three million.

Wilkins himself returned to the United Kindom in 1771, together with the civil servants of the East India Company who had made fortunes during their employment in India and who had come home to England very wealthy men. These people became known as the Nabobs and were thoroughly disliked. They rushed to enter Parliament thus putting up the price of seats and it was these Nabobs who became the landowners of England and Wales and by their manner became known as the landed gentry. Rumours were rife that these were the people responsible for the catastrophic famine in India, caused by those same company employees who had monopolised the rice crops, profiting greatly from the sale of grain, selling it at eight, ten, twelve times the price that they had paid for it.

On his return home to his native country, Walter Wilkins sought out a country house in which to establish his family life. He discovered and admired Maesllwych Castle and coveted that estate. He ascertained that it was originally owned by the Vaughns, but as the line had died out it passed through the daughter to Humphrey Howarth Esquire of Carbalfa in the Parish of Clyro. His son, Sir Humphrey Howarth Bart, had recently become involved in a contest to represent the County of Radnor in Parliament and, by other expensive pursuits, found himself financially embarrassed enough to mortgage his property to Walter Wilkins. Wilkins had, by then, become established at the Wilkins Bank in Brecon and in due course Wilkins foreclosed on the mortgage and purchased the estate of Maesllwych.

He then had erected on the site of the old house a new, large family mansion. Wilkins' substantial fortune was invested in the family banking business, which soon became a popular bank for the drovers and traders in the County and was the early forerunner of Lloyds Bank. It is still not exactly clear how Wilkins made his money while in India, but without doubt there was a remarkable rise in his fortunes. Maesllwych is an extensive estate of land with fishing rights on the River Wye, overlooking the village of Glasbury.

On 24 February 1777, Walter Wilkins married Catherine, the only daughter and heiress of Samuel Haywood of Walsworth Hall, Gloucester.

They had a son and named him Walter also. Wilkins Senior was a great social climber and it was essential to his ego that his family rated highly in the County and that his name was important and would remain so.

He was appointed Justice of the Peace for Radnor and in 1774 was High Sheriff. It was at this time that his thoughts centred around Westminster and he decided it was time he entered Parliament. There were two Members of Parliament for Radnorshire; one for the County and one for the Boroughs. The Boroughs consisted of New Radnor, Knighton, Knucklas and Radnor. Presteigne was the County candidate's seat. Walter Wilkins was eventually candidate for the County, his competitor was Thomas Johnes of Stanage who had resigned his seat for Cardigan and had offered himself for his father's old constituency of Radnor. This was bound to be a costly business, for his opponent was Wilkins.

Thomas Johnes' mother lived at Croft Castle, about eight miles from Presteigne on the Hereford side. The Dowager, as she was then styled, stated quite clearly that "try as he might, the Indian merchant would never be able to outdo her reckless son". This proved to be the case and, at enormous personal cost, Johnes was duly elected.

It was becoming clear in 1796 that Johnes was beginning to lose his way in social circles. He was accustomed to spending money in large sums and his debtors began to call in their dues. Eventually, the gossip in Herefordshire and the Border Counties caused Johnes to resign his seat for Radnor in the spring of 1796, stating that he was doing so

47

in order to stand as the next candidate for Cardiganshire in place of Lord Lisburn who was retiring. It was true that his main home was in Cardigan but in those days MPs did not lightly resign their seats, and relinquish the influence they gained from holding them, and it certainly appeared to be a strange thing for Johnes to have done. Wilkins eventually won the seat for the Whigs and held onto it continuously for thirty-two years.

An account paid to the Radnorshire Arms, Presteigne, shows that a bill exists for £466 and was presented to the candidate for fayre provided at election time; most of this cost being incurred during the last eight days of the campaign. The concluding item was dinner for 101 people, at which 117 bottles of sherry and 96 of port were drunk, as well as brandy and cider. It was an effective way of buying votes.

Walter Wilkins the Second appeared to be a strange young man, lacking in personality and always anxious to please his father. He too was thoroughly conversant in the ways of the upper classes and closely guarded his family background. Like his father, he enjoyed the social standing his name gave him in the County and indeed the Country. Despite his yearning for social status, Walter Wilkins the Second did not succeed to the title of High Sheriff of Radnorshire, unlike his ancestors and those who came after him, and there is no known reason for this. He was a member of Parliament, a position easily attained through his father's wealth and connections and he was also a Justice of the Peace, which allowed him certain powers.

In March 1806, he became engaged and
eventually married Catherine Devereux,
daughter of the Earl of Hereford, but they
left the County and went to live in London.
They had one son, Walter Wilkins the Third,
and three daughters; the first born was
christened Katherine Augusta Marianna, his
second daughter Mary Anne and his third
daughter Georgiana Frances. It is worth
noting that the name Mary was not considered
an upper class name at that time, it was a
name more usually associated with the servant
classes.

Maesllwych Castle became the social centre
for the upper classes of Wales and into it
flowed a constant stream of important visitors
who would come to stay with Walter Wilkins and
his most eminent family. They came to enjoy
their splendid style of hospitality and add to
the self-aggrandisement of Walter Wilkins and
his 'respected' lifestyle.

A likely guest at Maesllwych would be Mr
Justice George Hardinge the English Circuit
Judge for the Counties of Brecon, Glamorgan
and Radnorshire who, whilst on his official
visits for the English law courts, would
probably stop over when conducting the Assize
at Brecon. He was a distant relative of the
Wilkins family, as Mrs Wilkins was a cousin of
George Hardinge's mother through a distant
connection to Lord Camden. Hardinge was
always welcome and his powerful position in
legal circles and at the House of Commons
would have impressed Walter Wilkins Senior,
who would no doubt have seen in him a useful
friend and ally. George Hardinge had a
magnetic presence and his appearance and
reputation as a 'ladies' man would not have

gone unnoticed by the household servants and
staff.

In the spring of 1805, he might well have
been staying at Maesllwych before proceeding
to Brecon Court to conduct the trial of Mary
Morris, who had killed her child by cutting it
to pieces with scissors and burying it in the
garden at the house of the gentleman she
worked for. The Jury returned a verdict of
not guilty of murder and she was acquitted,
but she was sentenced to two years
imprisonment for concealment of the birth.
Following this trial, George Hardinge then
proceeded to Presteigne to conduct the Great
Sessions at the Shire Hall.

Some years previous to this, young Mary
Morgan came into service at Maesllwych Castle
and progressed to the position of undercook to
the Wilkins family. A connection at last.
Mrs Hardinge a cousin of Mrs Wilkins, George
Hardinge and Walter Wilkins Senior, and
Junior, both members of the same Westminster
Club (Parliament), young Walter courting the
Earl of Hereford's daughter and somewhere in
the middle Mary Morgan, described by the
newspapers of the day and by her Judge as
pretty, modest, intelligent and serious. She
was totally unaware of the fate that was
awaiting her under the roof of this "most
respectable Radnorshire gentleman".

It was back to the libraries again; the
target was the Judge. They told me he cried
on passing sentence and never came to
Presteigne without visiting Mary's grave.
Strange behaviour for a hanging Judge. It
made me wonder what Walter Wilkins had on him,
if indeed he had anything, and then the
telephone calls came. Late at night they

would intrude into my creative space, warning
me not to pry further into the matter of Mary
Morgan.  One caller even said that the curse
of Mary Morgan would be placed upon me.
Unsigned handwritten notes were pushed under
my door confirming the fact.  It was
unnerving, a feeling that my physical well
being was under threat . . . but from whom?
Why did it matter so much, so long after the
event?  Why the unease that filtered through
the locality whenever I asked a question?
What was the secret secret still keen to be
hidden?

Some notes were helpful, suggesting books to
read and listing certain facts.  It was as if
the town was ready to take me into its
confidence after all but not willing to be
exposed.  The older inhabitants recalled for
me tales told to them by their grandparents,
people who may have been around during Mary
Morgan's time in Presteigne.  When I touched
those old people I felt I was touching
history.  What a lovely thing to have done.
But it was time once again to start turning
the pages of history and get my fact finding
roadshow going again.  The facts I wanted were
the facts about Mr Justice George Hardinge MP
another 'respectable English gentleman' no
doubt.

The British Library was the next port of
call.  More reading, more researching, more
grist to this historical detective's mill.
George Hardinge was worth the long grind.

# CHAPTER SIX

## THE JUDGE

George Hardinge was born on 22 June 1743. He was the third son of Nicholas Hardinge and the eldest of those who survived. His father was a scholar and antiquary, clerk to the House of Commons and law reader to the Duke of Cumberland, eventually becoming Attorney General. In his final years he was appointed Secretary to the Treasury, a position he maintained until his death in 1758. In this capacity he was recognised as being able, zealous and so honest that he made many enemies. George Hardinge's mother was the daughter of Sir John Pratt and sister to Charles, First Earl Camden.

George Hardinge spent his early life at the family home Canbury, a manor house at Kingston-upon-Thames, where he was privately educated by a local schoolmaster. He later went on to Eton, under the Headship of Dr Barnard, and it was during this time be became an accomplished actor. At the age of fifteen his father died and George inherited the family estates but still continued his education. In 1761 he was admitted pensioner at Trinity College Cambridge and although he failed to sit his Arts Degree, eight years later he was given, by Royal Mandate, a Masters Degree in the same subject and began practising law.

George loved to move in literary circles, listing among his friend Arkenside the poet, John Nichols, Sir William Jones, Horace Walpole and Jacob Bryant. He also formed a close attachment to Anna Seward, a notable writer of her time, with whom he conducted a long correspondence over the years. Whether he had hopes of achieving a permanent relationship with the lady is questionable, as her romantic inclinations leaned very much towards members of her own sex. Nevertheless, they remained good friends.

George attracted women of all ages despite his short stature. His handsome looks appealed to them, which could have been the reason why Lady Gray, mother of Sir Charles Gray, financed his trip to Europe. She was ninety years old at the time.

On his return to England his law practice was neglected, which prompted a warning from his friend William Jones that he should, "Beware of wealth and pleasure". The full poem can be found in 'Chalmers Collection of British Poets' published in 1810. Taking the advice seriously, George Hardinge found himself a suitable wife in Lucy Long, heiress daughter of Richard Long of Hinxton, Cambridgeshire whom he married on 20 October 1777. They moved into Ragmans Castle, a small house in Twickenham next door to his friend Horace Walpole.

Unable to have children of their own, George and Lucy Hardinge adopted his nephew, the son of his brother Henry, and proceeded to educate him, making him their heir. He wasn't a bright boy at Eton, but he did distinguish himself in the Royal Navy, rising to the rank of Captain, his bravery gaining for him many medals and citations. He was awarded the Lloyds Sword for Gallantry at sea and his death in battle caused great distress to his adopted father.

53

After his marriage George's career progressed with distinction, becoming Solicitor General to Queen Anne and later her Attorney General. He was appointed counsel at the House of Commons and later the Lords. His performance whilst representing the East India Company, in opposition to Fox's India Bill, was masterly and prompted Lord Camden to say after hearing it, "I am able to pronounce upon my Judgement that in language, wit and voice, Hardinge has no superior at the Bar. His fortune is made, let him take care that he does not spoil it by levity and indiscretion."

In 1784 Hardinge was returned Member of Parliament for the pocket borough of Old Sarum in Wiltshire and held the seat until 1801. He was an eloquent and ingenious speaker with a rising reputation in Parliamentary and legal circles and his close friends indicated that "with a little discretion he cannot fail to make a considerable figure". However, many others felt that at the age of forty he was no longer a young man and it would be his indiscretion and levity that would prevent him reaching the front ranks of politics, the law and, for that matter, literature. His political leanings followed those of Lord Camden, his uncle, and Lord Pitt but he always preserved a measure of independence towards them.

With Lord Mansfield's resignation offering prospects of legal promotions, Lord Camden wrote, "If poor George should get a Welsh Judgeship in the scramble, he has not the spirit to push to anything greater. Is it not strange that he has fine parts and is the best speaker at the Bar, yet he will always be kept down below his merit because he does not know how to feel his own importance or to improve his capacity by discretion. I am sorry for it, he has a good many qualities and the best disposition in the world".

In August 1787, Hardinge was appointed Senior Justice of the Counties of Brecon, Glamorgan and Radnor. He was described as a painstaking Judge, an honourable and benevolent man who was witty and sprightly in manner. It is the same Welsh Judge whom Byron described as 'The Waggish Welsh Judge Jefferies Hardsman' in his poem 'Don Juan' Canton XIII Stanza 88.

"There was this waggish Welsh Judge
    Jefferies Hardsman,
  In his great office so completely
    skilled
  That when a culprit came for
    condemnation
  He had his Judge's Joke for consolation."

Hardinge enjoyed his life as Circuit Judge. Meeting and dining with influential people added to his feelings of self esteem. He was so pleased with his elaborate addresses to his condemned prisoners he always had them circulated to all the newspapers to ensure that his learned dissertations did not go unnoticed. His literary work was very important to him and he took it seriously, contributing to "Nichols' Literary Anecdotes and Illustrations", editing his father's writings and publishing his own letters, all of which can be found in his 'Miscellaneous Works' (three volumes) edited by his friend Nichols. Volume One contains his charges and speeches, Volume Two his verse writing, which according to Nichols was not worth printing, although the lighter poems were considered facetious and the serious, pleasingly impressive. Volume Three is his miscellaneous prose.

In his capacity as Vice President and early promoter of The Philanthropic Society, Hardinge raised over ten thousand pounds for charity and in 1769 he became a Fellow of the Society of Antiquaries and a Fellow of The Royal Society. He was acquainted with Walter Wilkins of Glasbury both in Parliament and on circuit and very likely through his investigation into the East India Company, whom he elected to defend at the Bar of the House of Commons.

Hardinge appeared to be a man who enjoyed the good life, acknowledging the attentions of the ladies and indulging in fine food and wine. During his years as a Judge, his hard attitude and unflinching ability to commit a person to the gallows stuck with him. His reputation preceded him; prisoners knew there would be no leniency from this Judge. He caused a stir wherever he went, was followed by a retinue of admirers among his own peers and generally relished the social standing his position gave him. He remained the Circuit Judge for Brecon, Glamorgan and Radnor until his unexpected death in 1816.

In April 1805, George Hardinge travelled to Presteigne to preside over the Great Sessions. He came with the reputation of a great lawyer and Judge, with high literary instincts and an impressive Parliamentary career. A man who, according to political commentators of the day, could have achieved even more greatness if he had not succumbed to flirtations of a literary nature, had a craving for money and the good life and an inability to recognise his own indiscreet behaviour. He was recognised as a tough, unbending Judge among the working classes but by his own kind a person to respect. Among the aristocracy, he was appreciated for his eloquence, wit and sparkling company, a description which, no doubt, George Hardinge enjoyed above all others.

Before this man, on 11 April 1805, came a seventeen year old servant girl to be tried for the murder of her bastard child. It was becoming less than a dog's chance for Mary Morgan. Sifting through the background material showed that she didn't stand a hope in hell. All the odds seemed stacked against her, but were they really? She had killed her baby but, as the evidence will show, it was a common enough crime and during my lost days in the archives at the National Library of Wales, many similar cases were listed.

The one meaningful digression I made, was to read up the trial of Mary Morris from Hay-on-Wye. It was similar to the Mary Morgan case. She had killed her unwanted child too, but the Jury found her not guilty of murder and she was sentenced to two years in prison for not registering the birth of her child. The 'less than a dog's chance' was now replaced with the real possibility of 'no answer' to the charge of murder. But wait, I bet Mary Morris' lover was not on her Jury! What went wrong then, for that pretty and innocent young girl who served well the Wilkins family and died because of it?

# CHAPTER SEVEN

## THE INCIDENT

As I said earlier, very little was known about Mary Morgan and the task of 'getting to know her' wasn't easy. I needed a break from the books and records and as Christmas 1978 was about due, what better time to relax. Friends had been invited for the holiday so it seemed the right time for a natural break. Christmas was usually spent away from Presteigne, with respective families, so my friend and I were looking forward to the festive season at home.

A single strand of coloured lights crisscrossed the High Street and the Coffee Pot window was duly decorated in preparation for the Chamber of Trade's annual competition for a silver cup which, I should add, I badly wanted to win but never did (although one year I really thought I should have done). Father Christmas arrived to switch on the lights and hand out parcels to the children on receipt of fifty pence. Jingle Bells poured out of an ageing gramophone and the Coffee Pot did a roaring trade on coffee and mince pies (locally made, of course).

Christmas Eve was a mixture of last minute shopping, lusty carol singers and a large scotch or two with Bill Sid the butcher, while he told me how he grew up on the adjoining estate to the De Wintons some fifty years previously. A pleasing discussion it turned out to be because, even on Christmas Eve, Mary Morgan sprung back at me as the bells of St Andrew's summoned one and all to leave the pubs, hostelries and log-fired hearths for the midnight service. And they did too: sober, drunk, non-conformist, catholic, the young and the old, the frail and the fit; all gathered for a Church of England service, in a Welsh Church with a Scottish name. I gave an amused wink at Mary Morgan's grave as everyone filed past it, on the way into church. Someone, somewhere, must have a clue to the secret secret of Presteigne.

Christmas came and went. New Year's Eve was almost a facsimile of Christmas Eve and as the bells rang out the old year, I strolled alone to the Lugg Bridge close by and stepped momentarily into my native England as the bell ringers happily rang in 1979. Stepping back into Wales again, I felt the gravestone calling me to it and, with the bells still pealing away, I purposefully walked across the churchyard, paused where I always pause and, with my left fist clenched tightly, said to Mary Morgan, "1979 is for us".

I was back on the road again, a road that took me to Llowes, a small village a few miles from Glasbury. I parked the car beside the church and although there was no-one to be seen, I felt they were all seeing me. I was aware that my every move was carefully monitored by countless pairs of eyes. As I entered the deserted churchyard, a chill passed through me despite my warm clothing but it wasn't the chill of a winter afternoon. The gate creaked as I opened it and I wanted to turn and run but I didn't. I wasn't going to let those unseen watchers smile at the fear of this coward; that would mean the unknown telephone callers were winning. The long grass was damp and beaten down as I intrepidly prowled among the old memorial stones of long passed on villagers. It seemed there were many other Morgans about at the time of Mary Morgan. The parish records would give me the details, so I made my way into the church porch to investigate further. The notice board listed the flower arranging rota, dates and times of services, church cleaning duties and the telephone number of the Vicarage.

I went inside the church. It was very clean, cold and empty . . . or was it? I'm sure the vestry door closed as I moved down the aisle; I heard the latch click. The chill struck again and a little voice inside me once more said, "Go for it Jen" and I did. This time straight out of the church door. I tried to look unconcerned as I left the churchyard but I'm sure I didn't and I departed the village without seeing a soul, but they saw me.

I phoned the Vicar that night and he told me that all parish records were now deposited in the archives at the National Library and it was back to Aberystwyth again. From my days there, studying the parish and trial records and mulling over the old newspapers, I was able to get a picture of the young woman's journey to the gallows at Presteigne.

Mary Morgan is thought to have been born on 30 March 1788, the daughter of Elizabeth and Reece Morgan of Llowes in the County of Radnorshire. Like other young girls of her day, she would have been sent into service at a suitable establishment near to her home, the choice likely made for her by her family.

Maesllwych Castle, situated at Glasbury-on-Wye, was such a place and Mary Morgan eventually took up a post as a member of the kitchen staff and, in time, she reached the position of undercook to the Wilkins family. She was described as pretty and intelligent, with a bright personality, a description which may have allowed her to become popular with her contemporaries. It is said that her young master, Walter Wilkins Junior, was 'taken with her'.

Life in the great house would have been hard and what free time she had may well have been spent visiting her family in Llowes and walking along the banks of the River Wye close by. Her duties at the Castle would have varied. Up early to light the fires, mixing and baking bread and pastry, preparing vegetables and occasionally killing and preparing a hen or two for the master's table.

During the spring of 1804, Mary would have been aware that she was pregnant. Documentary evidence suggests that the father of the child may have been a fellow servant or that she may have been seduced by her young master, Walter Wilkins Junior. Fearing for her job, it is unlikely that she would have exposed that fact. Therefore, she may not have confided in any of the other servants, although it is possible that she approached the male servant, suggesting that he may be responsible for her situation. A reference in a letter supports this and confirms that he offered to help her by 'giving her a herb which he had gathered and advised her to take it, which she was unable to accept, believing that it was intended by him to kill her child in the womb'. An offer of an abortion – that's interesting – and from someone who later denied being the father of her child.

The same document also shows that she appealed to her young master, ('whom yet she had indirectly accused of seducing her') for help and his response was very strange. He 'offered to maintain the child when born, if she would only say that he was the father', but Mary would not allow this. 'Such was her sense of honour, that although it would have saved her child's life, and her own, she would not purchase these two lives with a falsehood. "I determined to kill it poor thing, out of the way, being perfectly sure that I could not provide for it myself." These were her words and the substance of them was often repeated'.

It is important to stress at this point that these quotations have been extracted from correspondence between George Hardinge and the Bishop of St Asaph; detailed in a later chapter. But how odd that Walter Junior should want to claim the child as his, even though he said it wasn't, and whilst still courting the Earl of Hereford's daughter. Curiouser and curiouser!!

The style of dress in those days would have assisted her in keeping her condition a secret from the other servants while she considered the choice available to her. Some choice! To be cast out with her child, to beg, borrow or steal a living for them both, or to risk arrest and imprisonment as a vagrant and both left to die. Better one of us should live, she must have thought and thus she unknowingly planted the seed of her own destruction. Mary Morgan must have carried both her mental and physical burden entirely alone. No friends to confide in, no lover, intended or otherwise to support her through her weeks of concern and discomfort, no doctor at hand to ease her through her moments of pain, no social workers to share her worries. Yet she still must have worked a hard day in the kitchens, hiding her feelings of sickness and the evidence of her pregnancy from those close to her. All this she took upon herself, at the tender age of sixteen years.

On Sunday 23 September 1804 Mary Morgan was at her place of work. It was quite clear, from the evidence supplied at her trial by the other servants, that she was unwell. She had become ill during the early hours of the morning but she had managed to get up and work until about one o'clock in the afternoon, when she was advised by the other servants to go to her room and rest. During the course of the afternoon, she was visited by Mrs Simpson, the housekeeper, who brought to her warmed wine to ease the sickness. Between six and seven o'clock, the cook brought her some tea and yet no-one appeared to acknowledge her true condition.

Mary lay upon her bed, the advancing stages of labour upon her and throughout that fateful Sunday she must have realised the horrific ordeal she was to go through. Little did she know that she was embarking upon the most fearful journey of her young life. The afternoon was a series of interruptions from the other servants enquiring about her health, which she managed to parry. As her time came nearer, she somehow must have found the strength to lock the bedroom door and move a second bed against it. These exertions must have accelerated the final stages of labour, her obvious cries of pain and anguish unheard by those below. Unaided and alone, a very young girl delivered her unwanted child into a cruel and unwelcoming world.

The horror of this experience must have influenced her subsequent action. She knew what she had to do when she saw the small two-bladed penknife lying nearby. Had she placed it there herself or did someone leave it for her? The knife was valued at sixpence, a large sum of money for a servant girl to spend out of her meagre wage of two pounds per year! To suffocate the child would have been more fitting, but Mary Morgan killed her child in the only way she knew how. She attempted to sever the head from the body of her baby girl and then proceeded to hide the evidence of her crime in the mattress of her bed.

When Mary Meredith, the under dairymaid, went up to the room she shared with her friend Mary Morgan, it was clear that something untoward had happened. The bedroom door was locked and, despite her appeals to be let in, she was forced to call the other servants. Margaret Havard and Elizabeth Evelyn arrived on the scene and they both stated later, in evidence, that they challenged Mary to explain her condition and asked her if she had delivered a child. Again according to the evidence submitted, Mary cursed and swore, denying that such a thing had happened. They did not believe her and removing the bedclothes, saw for themselves the evidence of the birth and of the killing. Mary subsequently admitted to the fact and the Master of the household, Walter Wilkins Senior, was informed.

The atmosphere of death must have lingered in the passageways of the Castle, as the stale evidence of Mary's crime remained untouched amid the matted, bloodstained feathers of the underbed. The household awaited the arrival of Hector Appleby Cooksey, a coroner for the County of Radnor and one time landlord of the Radnorshire Arms, Presteigne. He had been called to examine the evidence and summon a Grand Jury to the scene, to enable committal proceedings against Mary Morgan to commence.

Mary Morgan, who would surely have been in a very frail condition and very frightened after the terrible ordeal she must have gone through, was eventually removed from the house of Walter Wilkins Esquire and escorted to the jail at Presteigne, the cost of her transportation payable out of whatever income she had.

So the deed was done and Mary had killed her unwanted child. Or was it wanted? Did she really want to kill it? Where did she get that penknife from? She could have more easily obtained a kitchen knife. Perhaps she even had second thoughts about killing her daughter and Mary Meredith banging heavily on the door may have pre-empted the act. So many questions, too few answers. Who was covering for whom? Only the trial would tell, or would it? As Bill Sid had said on Christmas Eve, "The gentry always sticks together no matter what". They stuck together all right, all the way to the gallows.

They took her to Presteigne to spend six months in the town's filthy, rat infested dungeons and on 11 April 1805, she appeared before her accusers at the Great Sessions of Wales to answer to a charge of murder before Mr Justice George Hardinge, Senior Justice of the Counties of Brecon, Glamorgan and Radnor, and associate of Walter Wilkins MP, her employer.

How I wish I could have defended her at her trial; no old boys' network would have stopped this middle aged woman from asking the right questions. All I could do was go back into the court at Presteigne, find a place in a corner and read the endless notes I had copied from the records and books, drifting back through time and listening to what went on.

George Hardinge – Judge of Mary Morgan
Portrait by N Dance
Photograph supplied by the
National Library of Wales

Jennifer Green - Judge of George Hardinge
Photograph supplied by The Hereford Times

# CHAPTER EIGHT

## THE TRIAL

It was a very warm day and the court was
empty. The caretaker let me in, chatted for a
while and left me to my thoughts. I wandered
around looking at, and touching, the wooden
dock with its brass rail and stood where she
had stood that fateful day. It wasn't the
same court that had housed the trial but a
good replica built on behalf of, and paid for
by, Walter Wilkins Senior not long after the
Mary Morgan affair. I stared at the Judge's
Bench, the Jury and witness boxes, the
pikestaffs on the wall and I wanted to shout,
"Bring in the Christians".

The bench I had chosen to sit on was at the
back of the public seating, at the end of the
row next to the wall. It was made of wood,
very hard, shiny and smooth from the countless
bottoms that had sat there before me. My box
files of notes were piled up beside me and I
began to sort the wheat from the chaff.

The ceremony of the Great Sessions at
Presteigne commenced on Monday 8 April 1805
and the trial actually started at three
o'clock the following afternoon. The
townsfolk of Presteigne would have been
excited and full of anticipation. In that
warm, close court room I could feel it too and
I was becoming aware of people filling up the
seating around me, a strong smell of flowers
and perfume invaded my thinking and I was
being taken over by an atmosphere that, until
now, I had only seen on paper. It washed all
over me and I closed my eyes and let it happen

as I floated back to the Great Session of Wales in the spring of 1805.

Outside, the streets were wet from the night rain and there was an air of hustle and bustle about the town. Armour and powder was being delivered to the Militia at the Garrison in Church Street and jugglers and acrobats performed to a motley collection of musical instruments. The customary carnival atmosphere had intruded into the normal lifestyle of the township as the County Town awaited the arrival of the judiciary. It was usual for the ladies to be dressed in their finery on these occasions, it was an afternoon's diversion for them, much appreciated by George Hardinge whose reputation as something of a 'ladies' man would have preceded him.

Conditions at the County Jail were an affront to justice. The small cell, no bigger than today's average coal shed, housed Mary Morgan plus other offenders. Straw was provided for sleeping and a loaf of bread per day was her ration of food, with ale provided from the jailer's tap if she could pay for it. It was dark in the dungeons, with no windows or candle light, except for an air brick let into the wall through which the occasional flicker of the jailer's rush light illuminated the cell. There would have been infestations of fleas and the visiting rats to share the claustrophobic cell with her as she endured these terrible conditions for over six months.

Throughout this period, Mary Morgan 'took it for granted that she would be acquitted and had ordered gay apparel to attest her deliverance, and supposed the young gentleman (presumably Walter Wilkins Junior) would save her by a letter to me' said the Judge in his letter to the Bishop.

Above her, in the court room, the public seating had been filled to capacity with little room for comfort. The presentations of flowers to the Judge's Bench added some colour to the drab courthouse and confirmed the adulation of the gentry for George Hardinge, seated on high, looking down onto the legal arena below. The press were jammed in the box provided for them, the likely increase in numbers due to a greater interest than was usual in such cases.

The twelve javelin men had assembled at their places inside and outside the Shire Hall. The counsellors, officers and the clerks were grouped together in the well of the court and Walter Wilkins Senior and his household sat in the area reserved for the notables of the town.

The Clerk of the Court called the Jury, the names drawn by lot from the jury box: Richard Price Esquire, MP of Knighton, Marmaduke Thomas Howell Gwynne Esquire of Llanalwedd, John Pritchard Esquire of Dolyfelin, John Bodenham Esquire of the Grove, Hugh Powell Evans Esquire of Noyadd, Samuel Lewin Pugh Esquire of Whitton, Charles Humphreys Price Esquire of New Radnor, Nathan Sedan Pritchard Esquire of Llandrindod, Thomas Howard Esquire of Knuclas, Richard Urwick Esquire of Walton, Thomas Pugh Esquire of Presteigne and Walter Wilkins Esquire, MP of Glasbury.

Twelve just men and true, selected from the gentry. Proud, rich and totally unmoved by the unfavourable comments from the public gallery that must have greeted the arrival of Walter Wilkins Junior, the accused's employer's son. News of the case would have travelled fast and, by now, it is likely that the townspeople were very much aware of the young girl in their jail and the details of her crime. The jailer would, no doubt, have leaked the story on his visits to the public house, for supplies of ale for himself and his tap system.

The Jury sworn in, the court was now ready to receive the alleged murderess. Every eye focused on the opening in the floor of the dock as Mary Morgan emerged from her six months in darkness into the sudden bright light of a spring day; like a lost mole breaking the surface of the earth for the first time. She was all that the newspapers and records had said, 'Her countenance was pretty and modest; it had even the air and expression of perfect innocence. Not a tear escaped her when all around were deeply affected by her doom; yet her carriage was respectful, her look attentive, serious and intelligent.' So said her Judge, who was also of the opinion that 'she had not the faintest conception of her crime'. She wore 'gay apparel to contest her crime' obviously quite sure that her young master would save her from the gallows. Nevertheless, it must have been a sad moment for her when she saw her fellow servants and friends who were to testify to her crime but an even greater shock to see young Walter Wilkins, of whom it appears she 'spoke with romantic affection', seated upon the Jury summoned to consider her fate.

At this point her confidence in her acquittal must have wavered; after all it is on record that 'she solicited her young master's help in the gift of a single guinea to her, for a counsel to do the best for her that he could'. He refused and later denied it all, but she did have a defender, paid for by the High Sheriff of the County 'in compassion to her desolate situation'.

I wanted to cry out, "You bastard, Wilkins". I wanted to urge the defender to challenge Jury, but none of my researches showed any record of a defence submission so I let it go. I could only sit and listen and watch.

With her in the dock were the three other defendants, all male, charged with stealing to a value of more than two pounds from a house, burglary and sheep stealing.

The court room settled down quietly as the Clerk stood up and read the charge. I followed his words from the copy in my notes.

"The jurors of our Lord the King, on their oath charge you, Mary Morgan, spinster late of the Parish of Glasbury in the County of Radnor, that on the 23rd day of September in the 44th year of the reign of our Sovereign Lord George the Third by the Grace of God and the United Kingdom, Great Britain and Ireland King, Defender of the Faith, that being big with child on that same day and year, at the home of Walter Wilkins Esquire of the Parish of Glasbury in the County of Radnor, by the providence of God you did bring forth a female child from your body alone and in secret, which being born alive was, within the laws of the land, a bastard.

You, Mary Morgan, not having the fear of God before your eyes, but having been moved and seduced at the instigation of devil on that day mentioned and in that

same place used force and arms upon that
female child and feloniously, wilfully
and with malice aforethought did assault
her with a certain penknife, the value of
that penknife being sixpence. Holding
that certain knife in your right hand,
you then and there made an assault upon
your bastard child with such forceful
striking and cutting upon her throat and
neck, enough to deliver a mortal wound of
the breadth of five inches and a depth of
two inches. The said child then and
there died instantly. The jurors so
sworn at your committal swore that you,
Mary Morgan, did feloniously, wilfully
and with malice aforethought kill and
murder against the peace and dignity of
our Lord the King. Witnesses will be
called before you to verify the charge."

For such a young and uneducated girl, the
proceedings of the court would have been
beyond her comprehension and understanding. I
cry for her sometimes, at what she had to go
through.

The Judge called the first witness. It was
Hector Appleby Cooksey, Coroner for the County
of Radnorshire and Landlord of the Radnorshire
Arms, Presteigne. He made his way through the
bulging court room to the witness box,
disregarding the ribald comments from the
public seated at the back of the court, many
of whom were most likely his customers. With
his face red, more from his drinking habits
than from embarrassment, he climbed the steps
to the witness box and stood erect, though
slightly in awe before the Judge. I had the
feeling from those around me that he wasn't

too comfortable as he read his statement to the court.

"On the 25th day of September last, I was summoned most urgently to the house of Walter Wilkins Esquire of Glasbury to examine events that had occurred there two days previous. Upon my arrival at the household, I was taken to view the body of a new born female child, delivered in secret, by a servant of the household. I summoned to meet me there one Thomas Bevin Esquire and twelve other just and lawful men of the said County and duly chosen and who agreeing then and there duly sworn and charged to enquire for our Sovereign Lord the King, by what means the new born female child came to her death, do upon their oath say that Mary Morgan late of the Parish of Glasbury in the County aforesaid (a single woman), did on the 23rd day of September of the year aforesaid being then and there big with the said new born female child afterwards to wit on the same day and year at the Parish aforesaid in the County aforesaid, delivered the said female child alone and secretly from her body and by the Providence of God did bring forth alive a female child which by the laws and customs of this Kingdom, was a bastard and that the said Mary Morgan not having the fear of God before her eyes but moved and seduced by the instigation of the devil, afterwards to wit on the same day and year, at the Parish aforesaid, with force and arms upon the said new born female child, so alive and in the Peace of God and our

Lord the King, then and there being feloniously wilfully and of her malice aforethought, did make an assault and that the said Mary Morgan, with a certain penknife made of iron and steel of the value of sixpence. Which the said Mary Morgan there, had held in her right hand the throat of the said female child and feloniously, tratiously, wilful and with malice aforethought, did strike and cut and that the said Mary Morgan with the penknife aforesaid by the striking and cutting did then and there give to her said female child one mortal wound of the length of three inches and the depth of one inch from which mortal wound her said female child then and there instantly died. And so the foreman of the said jury for himself and fellows do say the said female child came to her death not otherwise. In Witness whereof the said Coroner, as the said foreman of the said Jurors on behalf of himself and the rest of his said fellows in their presence, have to this inquisition with their hands and seals the day year and place above mentioned."

Cooksey stared at the Judge and as he left the box, he drew from the top pocket of his gaudy chequered jacket, a blue spotted pocket handkerchief. Very carefully, he mopped his now sweating brow and returned to his seat.

The atmosphere was warming up as the court room took in the evidence of the Coroner. Their restlessness ceased at the calling of the first witness Elizabeth Evelyn, cook to the household. Her normally warmhearted outlook was lost in the nervous tensions of the occasion. Not being able to read or write, the statement she had made had been written down for her at the committal proceedings and was now read out loud on her behalf. I again took my copy and followed the reader.

"Elizabeth Evelyn, cook to Walter Wilkins Esquire of Maesllwych in the County of Radnor deposeth that on Sunday morning the 23rd September 1804 her fellow servant Mary Morgan, under cook to the above Walter Wilkins Esquire, was taken ill about two o'clock in the morning and continued her work till near one o'clock (the following afternoon) when she went to bed. About three o'clock in the afternoon Mrs Simpson the housekeeper gave her some warm wine, between six and seven she had some tea when the witness left her. About half an hour after she returned and found the said Mary Morgan in bed (who lay upon two beds) and then charged the said Mary Morgan with having delivered herself of a child (from some particular circumstances which she saw). She strongly denied it for half an hour or thereabouts and then owned up she had delivered herself of a child which was in the under bed, cut open among the feathers with the head nearly divided from the body, supposed by a penknife which was found by the witness bloody, under the same bed the morning following, being Monday the 24th of September 1804." Witness the mark of Elizabeth Evelyn.

A cross was placed alongside the name. She left the box without looking at Mary and returned to her seat with the Wilkins family.

Next to give evidence was Margaret Havard and her statement was also read out to the Court. I again followed along with notes.

"She came to Walter Wilkins to a first cook in the place of Mary Morgan who was taken ill on Sunday the 23rd September 1804. She saw her about four of the clock in the afternoon being then very ill. Returning to her between six and seven of the clock then charged her with being like a woman in labour which she strongly denied and was very angry at being asked the question. She desired the cook not to suffer any person to attend unto her for an hour as she thought she could sleep. Her door being described to be fastened alarmed the witness when she returned with the cook and then charged Mary Morgan of having delivered herself of a child, then she strongly denied it with bitter oaths for some time when she owned up that she had delivered herself of a child which was in the underbed cut open, deep sunk in the feathers with the child's head nearly divided from the body, supported by a pen knife which was found by the cook bloody under the pillow of the same bed the next morning following, being Monday the 24th of September 1804." Witness the mark of Margaret Havard.

The final witness was Mary Meredith, the under dairymaid who shared the attic bedroom with Mary Morgan. She must have seemed

76

frightened at giving evidence against her friend. The statement was read out for her.

"She swore that she was Under Dairymaid with Walter Wilkins Esquire at Maesllwych in the County of Radnor and that returning home from a visit to her sister on Sunday evening the 23rd of September 1804, she went upstairs to change her clothes, to the room that Mary Morgan was in (she being in the habit of sleeping in the said room with the said Mary Morgan but not in the same bed) when she found the door fastened. She called to Mary Morgan to open the door which she refused and desired the said witness to go down as she thought she could have some sleep." Witness the mark of Mary Meredith and her mark was shown.

Thus was laid against Mary Morgan the evidence of her friends. All very conclusive, all written down by the same hand, (very likely the Clerk to Cooksey) and all sworn as correct and signed with the cross of the illiterate, all three employed by the same man who was also the employer of Mary Morgan.

No-one appears to have questioned that fact. What was the defender going to do about it, apart from taking the fee? A statement for the defence must have been made on Mary Morgan's behalf but there is no record of it, so I walked across the court room to where the defender was seated and offered him my defence, the one I would have delivered had I been her defender and based entirely upon my researches and my feelings. Against the silent wishes of that humbug of a Judge, he studied it and then rose from his seat.

A speech for the defence was such a rare occurrence that there was silence in the entire court room, not even the rustle of a skirt or movement of a foot could cut through the air of anticipation that hung between the four walls of the court house. He spoke slowly and clearly.

"Conditions exist throughout this land, more so in this rural part of Wales, under which young women, especially those engaged in domestic service, are left to fend for themselves after having been seduced, usually by their betters and often by their employers or the employer's family."

Hardinge looked uneasy but the defender hesitated long enough only to allow a contrived cough from the public seating, that seemed to acknowledge collective agreement of the defender's suggestion. He went on.

"This poor girl, victim of such a situation and fearing for her position in domestic service, took it into her head to secretly deliver herself of an unwanted child with the intention of concealing it from authority. Being young and inexperienced, totally unaware of the pitfalls, dangers and illegalities of such an act, she prepared herself for the ordeal of her young life. She took herself into the peace and quiet of her own room and there, in the solitude, she set about the awesome task of delivering her baby. Racked with pain and suffering and confused with the worries of finding support and maintenance for her bastard child, the wanderings of her mind took her from reality into fantasy. She stumbled in mind and thought and entered the fear stricken world of despair and disaster. She could not care for her child in isolation and unable to recognise right from wrong, took the only course open to her in so desparate a situation. She killed the child after its birth, the child she could not afford to keep. This is not uncommon and is frequently carried out by young women finding themselves in the same position as this poor, unfortunate girl. As the law stands at present, concealment of a birth is punished by only two years imprisonment at the most. A similar case in Brecon occurred last week and received the same considerations. Examination of the case histories will bear witness that this crime exists rarely in the upper classes, is surely the vice of the poor and generally of those in domestic service. There has not been a conviction at the Old Bailey for this type of charge for the last two decades; even the existence of trials for this offence is very limited. I do not question the seriousness of the charge brought before this Court, I only plead that just consideration be given to the nature and circumstances of the offence and that the examination of the crime of Mary Morgan be considered alongside those of a similar type. I ask that the charge of murder be stricken from the sheet and be replaced by concealment of a birth."

There was a hush in the Court, the restlessness of the public gallery had broken the stillness of the oppressive court room as the townsfolk nodded in agreement. Greater emotion now was present in the voice of Mary Morgan's defending counsel.

"In God's name, it is less than this poor creature deserves after her long ordeal of imprisonment in the filthy, black hole this town calls its jail. She has surely suffered enough and paid the price already.

I ask you, My Lord, and you, the Jury, to give heed to this entreaty, consider my judicious pleadings and look upon this contrite figure in the box. Allow her the mercy of your intelligent minds before finally judging her weakness and at the same time, let us examine our own context. That is all my Lord."

The defence counsel sat down to sporadic clapping from the public gallery and then turned to look at me. I nodded my thanks for his effort.

It must have been an uncomfortable moment for the Judge, for the Wilkins Family and for the assembled gentry. The servants, who had given evidence against Mary Morgan, sat in silent conflict as the Court waited for the Judge to commence his address to the Jury before despatching them to consider a verdict. The Judge ordered a break for refreshments, which allowed me the time to absorb the atmosphere and feeling that now invaded my imaginations.

The court room relaxed and the people began to chat together, as the Judge took a drink handed to him by his Clerk. He chatted to the people close to him and waved to members of the Jury. Walter Wilkins Junior was looking very uncomfortable in the Jury box, his father looking directly at him nodded across the court room. One or two gentlemen seated at the back of the court room were in deep conversation, heads together like secret conspirators. The servants who had given evidence against Mary Morgan, sat in silent conflict in the seats provided for them. The public gallery was restless, waiting in anticipation for the Judge to continue.

The members of the Jury stretched themselves and resettled for the address. They expected it to be hard and to the point and they were not disappointed. There was to be no deviation from his usual style.

Hardinge stood and stretched also, brushed himself and settled down back in his wide, wooden seat. Readjusting his wig, he looked directly at Mary Morgan who returned his gaze with a directness which must have caused him cold discomfort. He turned quickly and fixed his gaze upon the jury, took another sip from his cup and cleared his throat. He surveyed his audience and in his well-known sonorous tones gave vent to his feelings on the matter. But were they entirely his?

"Gentlemen of the Jury, in addressing you I call upon humane and public spirited men for their help in painful trust which is apportioned between us. You are interposed by the constituence of this merciful Government, as friends and guardians of liberty and of innocence, and you have made a compact, though by tacit, agreement with the prisoner accused before you who is unheard in her defence and personated only by the evidence against her and the voice of her defender."

81

The Judge paused, Mary continued to look at him. Her fellow prisoners in the dock with her began to look bored and disinterested. Hardinge carried on.

"You have also made a covenant of a more elevated kind with a God of truth, whose Ministers, gentlemen of the Jury, you are and in whose presence we have a very solemn oath. What is that covenant? It is to be merciful if we can, to be firm if compassion is perjury and a violation of your trust."

Hardinge's voice began to rise at the sound of his own words and after some thought, he continued.

"I am to address men so described upon a subject of a most unlawful and melancholy nature, it is upon the guilt of murder, the culprit, and one's heart bleeds at the recital, is a girl whose age of seventeen is annexed and the victim, as alleged a new born child, her own illegitimate offspring, born as well as conceived in shame, but therefore making with its infant cries a more eloquent appeal to the mercy of that female parent, as well as to the fond impulse of maternal attachment which cannot be separated from the essence of her office, and implanted by the parent of us all in her bosom."

The gentlemen of the press were beginning to write, their interest was carried towards the public gallery and they, too, were becoming involved in, if not completely understanding, the words of the Judge. A slightly effeminate ring was beginning to sound in the tones of

Judge Hardinge as he continued his long discussion with the Jury.

"Whatever shades of mitigation the God of infinite mercy, in the counsels of his unfathomable wisdom should have destined for this class of murder, which bears not the least analogy to other homicide, the laws of the realm have made no distinction of mercy in its favour."

He directed his next words to the defending counsel:

"They were, and for near two centuries, more severe upon women accused of this crime than for men accused of any homicide whatsoever. It was the enacted provision of the law that concealment of the birth on the part of the female parent should operate as proof that she was guilty of the murder imputed, if she could not prove that the child was born dead."

The three gentlemen at the back of the hall who had previously been huddled together began to take more interest in the words of the mighty Judge. Hardinge looked straight at them and went on speaking.

"This enacted law was recently done away with, but I, who will yield in principles of mercy to none, am not yet right for the conclusion that, arraigned as it has often been for its cruelty, but administered as it was by the judges in that spirit of mercy which is vital to their branch of office, it was not salutary in the terror of it. I am not ready also for the conclusion that, as the law is now understood, sufficient care has been taken of the helpless

83

child, who as the offspring of incontinence or seduction is brought secretly into the world."
He placed his hands upon his bench and breathed deeply for a moment or two.

"Cases occur to me, but I will not point them out, in which the murder would escape. Distinctions, however, still prevail which are powerful barriers against this painful crime. The concealment of a birth is material evidence against the mother, because it indicates the wish to guard against the shame of the illegitimate birth. It is however, though competent and material as far as it extends, presumptive grounds of inference. This can be counteracted by another presumption which is that nature would prompt the mother to save her infant's life though desirous to conceal its birth. If it stood upon these two presumptions alone, the merciful one is the safest and perhaps in philosophy is the most correct of the two."
At this point his voice dropped.

"In truth however, these contending presumptions on both sides depend chiefly for their weight upon a due and sound comparison to the other leading facts in the evidence before us."
The Judge's Clerk was writing furiously. It was always his job to make detailed notes of any of Judge Hardinge's speeches, as the Judge himself was keen to have them circulated to all literary outlets and a copy despatched to the Editor of the 'Cambrian' newspaper.

Hardinge turned, after some thought, to the Jury.

"Your province, in general, is to enquire if the culprit was the mother of a living child, and robbed that infant of its life either by her own hand with a desire to kill it, or by an act both wilful and criminal which has killed it in effect. I take this opportunity of stating the latter example in mercy to other young women who may have been seduced into the delivery of an illegitimate offspring in secret. These young women are to know, that if they expose their child when living and it suffers death or if they deprive it wilfully of sustenance in their power to bestow upon it and it perishes, they commit as palatable a murder of the child as if their own personal hand had inflicted the death wound. But in so dreadful a penal case you must be thoroughly convinced that life that previously existed was destroyed by a wilful act of the parent, either as the act of killing it, or as an act which must in its nature have been calculated for that end result, whether intended for it or no. This inference may be collected from circumstances without ocular evidence to the living child or by the mother's crime of killing it."

Hardinge stopped, and leaning forward, took the cup and drank from it again. He was beginning to look tired and perhaps felt he was not making himself clear enough in some quarters. A thoughtful furrow creased his now ageing brow.

"I put one case for illustration: if the child is found in the necessary with

no marks of external violence, and where
no evidence appears against the mother,
except her concealment of the birth, it
has often happened that she has been
acquitted because women are liable to the
accident of a delivery there, which has
perfectly unabled them to save the
infant. It is certainly no legal excuse
that fear of the consequences, remorse of
the illegitimate birth or a sense of
delicacy and of shame were the motives to
so desparate an extremity, if stings of
this kind can be called frenzy of the
moment, they cannot escape unless they
have obliterated all traces of moral
distinction between right and wrong. If
any such case appears, you will act upon
it, but it would be a dangerous and false
mercy to infer it as of course and
presume it."
He paused again, which gave me time to look
about. The Jury were beginning to look
bemused by all the words. Walter Wilkins
Junior still had not lifted his head from his
chest and the pikemen guarding the prisoners
in the dock were looking jaded. The Judge's
supporters were trying their best to look
impressed, but his lady admirers gathered
round his bench were utterly bored. Everyone
knew that they were in for a long dissertation
by a Judge who so loved his own words.
Hardinge was unmoved by the general feeling of
boredom; his voice rambled on.
"Confessions of the parties accused are
too often received in these cases, when
they have been most unduly obtained by
menace or by the artificial tampering
with hope."

He glared at the defending counsel and then turned again to the Jury.

"I conjure you to repel all confessions thus obtained. Many are the cases where the influence cannot in strictness be called external, but results from the situation itself. I should be happier for one, if no party accused could be heard before this time. I must however add that confessions however obtained, if they terminate in discoveries of the fact, are competent as leading to such discoveries, and are no bars to the weight of the facts so discovered.

There is a familiar experiment in these cases upon the lungs of the child when detached from the other subjects of the dissection. I have no judicial knowledge whether it has been made in the case before us or has been omitted. It should always be made and for this reason, the result as evidence against the culprit is equivocal and I should never deem it improper to be received, but, if the lungs had sunk, it would have been decisive to show that it was a child still born, for which reason the poor creature in your hands had a just claim to the benefit of the experiment in her favour. I, for one, am so confident upon that subject that upon the fact of such an experiment and result, I would at any time encourage enough to direct an acquittal."

The tension in the court was interrupted by noise and the sounds of fireworks in the street outside. A crowd had gathered outside the Shire Hall and raised, chanting voices continually interfered with the Judge's address. He stopped speaking and indicated to the pikemen to investigate. They immediately adopted an attitude of control and made a hurried exit from the Court. This unexpected interval allowed a moment of relaxation in the overcrowded court room and the people packed tightly alongside me in the public seating nudged and conferred with each other on the Judge's words so far. Whether or not they understood them was immaterial, the great Mr Justice George Hardinge had been speaking.

The reporters in the press box reviewed their notes, agreeing or disagreeing, depending on their bias towards Hardinge. He was always a favourite with their editors and provided a constant source of news. The atmosphere in the room was heavy; the once scented air had now been erased by a more basic aroma of perspiring bodies.

Mary Morgan stood in the same position as she had done throughout the trial, her hands clasping the brass railing in front of her, still and pensive, making no effort to recognise her friends or accusers.

The noise outside had quietened considerably and the pikemen returned to join the others surrounding the dock. Hardinge brought the Court to order once again. He had no intention of his words being lost in unnecessary chattering.

"The appearance and state of the wound, if any wound was ever inflicted, are material circumstances as indicating life since the birth and accident or design is the cause of death. There is one peculiarity in this class of murder, it is nothing, or it is murder, it cannot be

88

justified, it cannot be a case of self defence, it cannot have risen from provocation and therefore it cannot be manslaughter, but it is these very peculiarities which heighten the merciful presumption that a mother would feel her natural impulse to her child which presumption is counteracted however, in some degree by the other which I have intimated, viz that which arises from her fear and shame. Character here is at best equivocal, and it may encourage the inference that for the sake of preserving this character, the guilt was incurred. It is a most painful dilemma to the best feelings of the heart when cases like these come before us."

The Judge's voice seemed to unexpectedly break slightly at that point, but he recovered himself and continued.

"But we must not overlook the danger of impunity, the compassion which is due to others whom the escape of this culprit may seduce, or the solemn oath that we have taken to be just."

He paused again, waiting for his words to fall on the ears of the Jury ensuring that they were absorbed in all of them.

"I am not afraid of telling that, offences like this are of late becoming prevalent, and that a culprit has recently escaped from her doom, whose crime was in local vicinity and was near to the scene of this."

The entire court became immediately interested in what was being said. The defence counsel pulled himself together and the Jury looked at one another keenly. The press reporters were poised ready for the explanation.

"It will on the one hand induce you to be firm, if the exingency is imperative but it will guard you against all prejudice resulting from the policy of example. We must not redress the unjust opportunity of yesterday by the over strained convictions of a similar offence today."

The Judge ended his address to the Jury concerning Mary Morgan and turned his attention to the three other offenders in the dock with her and briefly, but clearly, advised them of the charges against them and indicated to the Jury their collective duty towards all the prisoners before them. There was little interest shown in the Judge's words concerning the other three defendants and at the end of the address Hardinge guided the Jury, in a voice bold and confident, as to their duty to Mary Morgan.

"I consign this life into your hands without fear, convinced we shall hear of her no more as a criminal, if you are not sure of her guilt and I am convinced no less, that if you are thoroughly possessed of her guilt, no effeminate and vitious mercy, will shake the public spirit and courage of your trust. Go now and consider your verdict."

The silence was broken only by the collective breathing of the gathering. Mary did not move. The gentlemen of the press were momentarily captivated by the enigmatic beauty of the young girl accused of such a brutal crime. Their pens seemed no longer motivated to write. It was as if her silent unmoving posture had challenged the hard seasoned pressmen to criticise her actions. The unprepared-for pause irritated George Hardinge, he was not used to silent insubordination in his court room. He beckoned with an extravagant flourish to the Clerk of the Court who rose and led the Jury from the box and out of the court room.

It didn't seem to take long. They returned and the Judge enquired if they had reached a verdict. They all had. Each and every one of them found her guilty of murder.

I reacted badly to the verdict and wanted to stand up and challenge all that had gone before. No-one seemed to care about the injustice of it all and a feeling of great sadness welled up inside me as I buried my face in my hands knowing, as I did, the final outcome. The town reacted badly too. After all, Mary Morris was acquitted in Brecon only the week before, tried in front of the same Judge and acquitted. They knew what was going on too and they couldn't stop it.

Another firework exploded in the street as Judge Hardinge prepared to address the prisoner. I had my copy ready too, just in case I needed to make a gesture of defiance at some point. The Judge called for order once again. Mary Morgan stood, her face ashen at the turn of events but she faced her Judge still convinced she would not hang. George Hardinge looked long at Mary Morgan, his face had lost its normal composure, highlighted by a muscular twitching around his cheek bones. The Jury were fidgeting, not daring to look at the girl they had declared guilty. The press anxiously awaited the second delivery that was surely to come from the learned Judge.

Hardinge was nervous and tense, his eyes attempting to rest on anyone but the girl before him in the dock. He waited, as if seeking the words that he wished to deliver to her and he cast a long look at Walter Wilkins Senior before commencing his address to the poor helpless girl. With a tremble in his voice, quiet in comparison to the earlier speech, and breathing deeply as if struck by some asthmatic affliction, he sought to control his emotions.

"Mary Morgan upon evidence which leaves not a shade of doubt upon the mind, you are convicted of murdering your child, a new born infant of your own sex, the offspring of your secret and vicious love. You are convicted of murdering this child with a knife, deliberately selected as the implement of a purpose deliberately formed and before your infant came into the world. You could not hate the victim of this murder, it never offended you. It is true, if it had lived it would have proved your crime in its birth and your shame would have been the consequence of that proof. Was this a reason to kill it, if its first cries to you for sustenance and care made it by force a living accuser of your guilt and infamy?

Had it lived you might have lost your place, you might have lost other places, you might have lived in poverty as well as shame, but was this a reason to kill it. Was it a reason to acquire a false character and flourish in the world with a guilty conscience upon your pillow and cries of a murdered infant in your ear?

When did this fear of shame and poverty begin? Was it an obstacle in the way of your criminal intercourse with your lover? No! When you had criminal passions to indulge, you had no fear of risk. When those passions were satiated and the mischief had been done, you became a coward and sacrificed your infant offspring's life, as well as the interest of your soul hereafter, to that new born fear."

Mary Morgan gripped the rail again, as the realisation of Harding's words became clearer. She appeared unbelieving at what was happening to her.

"Alas, how dreadful are the landing places of the guilt when it ascends in its progress. You began with incontinence, criminal in itself, but full of complicated perils in its tendency to worse crimes. Your next guilt was a mask to the world in the concealment of your pregnancy, which, besides the sin of the imposture, was dangerous to the infant you had conceived and your last crime was the murder of your child inflicted by yourself.

You have killed the human creature, whom of all others had the most affecting right as well as claim to your mercy and love. You have murdered the offspring of your own guilt entailed by the shame of its descent upon her innocent life. At your wild and youthful age, undisciplined by fear as well as unenlightened and with such early habits of depraved self indulgence, it is not probable that a religion, which breathes in every page of it the love to infants, could have been impressed upon your mind, but the God of Nature has written a book which he that runs may read. You have read that book and the letters of it were stamped upon your feelings at your birth. It was a written law upon the living tablets of the heart, which told you how unjust it was to punish the offspring of your own guilt for no offence but the wretched life you had forced upon it, by that guilt alone."

Hardinge paused again and the silence was astounding.

"You should have exerted every moment of your own life in atoning, by redoubled affection to daughter so born, for the calamity of such an existence. Instead of projecting this atonement, you were deaf to her infant cries, and stifled her breath with a murdering hand, but in this choice of difficulties, in this conflict of chance and risk, what is it you have done?"

He looked directly at Mary Morgan.

"You have taken a leap in the dark, you have encountered the peril of detection and of punishment by death, as the murderer of your child."

I looked at the girl in the dock; for the first time Mary's impassive, pale face allowed the shadow of fear to pass across it. She looked desperately at her defender, he looked away. The Judge's voice cut through my thoughts.

"You took the chance of dying impenitent - which God avert - or with a conscience ill-prepared for so dreadful a change as from this life, at once into eternity and its judgements. You took the chance and had you escaped from human detection, had you imposed upon the world ever so well, of living self-accused, and self-accused upon a bed of lingering torments. Thus is it that one guilt produces another, especially in your sex when seduced into its criminal intercourse with ours."

His voice broke at this point and he coughed, for what seemed to be too long a time to satisfy the mounting curiosity of the gathering. His composure regained, the Judge progressed with his line of so-called reasoning.

"The natural delicacy of the female character entangles all its progressive guilts and a succession of crimes take their birth from the master key to them all, your dread of shame. At last the mind is buried in the confusion of shifted expedients to escape from the importunate eye of the world, but there is an eye about the path and about the bed, from which no darkness can escape and from which nothing is hidden. That eye is never closed, and it brings guilt like yours into light, in a manner for which human conjecture despairs to account. Guilt is always a coward, guilt like yours often prompts the sinner to accuse himself and prove his crime by other evidence of the fact in a fit of despair, surprise or fear. Madness like this comes too late. It is the effect and the doom of guilt, but it is no shelter from it."

Hardinge's voice petered out. I watched him closely as he put his hand to his head and smoothed his temples with his thumb and fingers. He passed his hands gently across his brow, in an attempt to shield his watery eyes from the silent queries of the anxious onlookers. Aware of the prolonged hush, he leaned back nervously and carried on.

"You had no plea of sudden impulse to this act, not that any such plea could avail you if it existed. Yours was a deliberate murder, the deadly implement was procured and set apart for that purpose. Had you escaped, many other girls thoughtless and light as you have been, would have been encouraged by that escape to commit your crime in hope of your impunity. The merciful terror of your example will save them. Desperate acts like these often escape from punishment. Merciful juries, merciful rulers of law and merciful judges give occasion to that impunity. If it is a defect I hope it will never be repaired but the same juries, the same law and the same judges are firm in their trust in cases like yours. The life that you destroyed lost its mother when you were its executioner for guilt of your own. But it found a parent in heaven. There is not a more sacred object than that parent's love, whose children we all are, than a new born child. Its blood is like that of Abel; it cries from the earth and that cry is heard upon His throne in whose image your murdered child was created."

Hardinge looked as if he was beginning to feel the effects of his tiredness. All eyes in the court were upon him, awaiting his next move. He looked across at Wilkins Senior who did not return his glance. He then slowly passed his eyes across the faces of the Jury and came to Wilkins Junior, whose head was still bowed. Hardinge's supporters were subdued, the ladies sitting either side of him, normally rejoicing at his words, were unnaturally quiet. I was completely overwhelmed by the experience.

The streets outside echoed the silence, muted as though time had stood still. Despite all his inner thoughts, his Lordship continued.

"What your inducement was to sacrifice this pledge of your love with your crime, we have no power to ascertain, your conscience knows it, but we are able to know that it must have been unjust and cruel.

I have talked with you hitherto as a Judge, going to pass a sentence of death upon his convicted prisoner before him. But look up to me and I can give you comfort, for I can tell you without impairing the weight of your punishment in this world, that you can turn away your eyes to the Judge of us all, whose mercy has no limits and whom no sinner can implore in vain, appealing to Him with tears of penitence and remorse, if they are deep and sincere. You must have expected your fate and I hope in God you have prepared yourself by a new made

heart for a better world, having made all
the human atonement in your power upon
earth."

The entire court room was hanging on to the
words of the Judge, who paused and brought
from inside his flowing robes a large
handkerchief. He blew his nose and moved as
if to wipe his eye. Clearing his throat he
spoke again.

"To cut off a young creature like you
in the morning of her day, for it is a
little more than a day to the oldest of
us all, is an affliction thrown upon me
which I have no power to describe, or to
bear so well as perhaps I should."

His voice was almost contrite as he
delivered, what was to me, his most
unforgettable comment.

"You must not think we are cruel, it is
to save other infants like yours and many
other girls like you, from the pit into
which you are fallen."

George Hardinge collapsed in uncontrolled
sobbing, tears rolled down the venerable face
of the eminent protector of law and order; he
dabbed at them with the ends of his long wig.
His elderly Clerk looked at him in utter
amazement, the learned counsels were staggered
and the press men wrote with immense speed in
an effort to capture in words this incredible
scene. The general public were agog at the
sight but the mood was abruptly broken by a
hysterical titter from one of the lady
admirers. Mary Morgan absorbed it all in
total isolation.

Hardinge collected his thoughts. After one
final blow of his bulbous nose, he accepted
again the task in hand.

"Your sentence is a mercy to them. If you have repented your crime, it is a mercy to yourself. Had you escaped, your mind perhaps would have been so depraved that mercy could not have reached it in time.

You have the tears and prayers of us all, in the abhorrence of your crime we have not lost compassion for your personal fate, nor our hope that you will find mercy at the judgement seat of a redeeming intercessor who died, that penitent sinners through him should be rescued from the doom they had incurred and should expiate their pollutions in the atonement of his blood."

Mary stood in the dock, a lone figure, her body limp as she tried to listen and understand what was happening to her. Hardinge placed the black square of linen upon his bewigged head. In a voice so distressed that his words could hardly be heard, he passed sentence upon Mary Morgan.

"I am now to pass upon you, the awful sentence of your legal and inevitable fate in this world. It is, that you be taken from hence to the place from whence you came and from thence to the place of execution the day after tomorrow. You are there to hang by the neck until you are dead; your body is then to be dissected and anatomised. But your soul is not reached by these inflictions. It is in the hand of your God! May that fountain of love show mercy to it when it shall appear before him at the day of judgement."

A moment of panic fleeted across Mary's face
as she heard the sentence, but she still
appeared unaffected by her certain fate. All
those around me in the public seating were
stunned by the sentence and I sat among them
and struggled to come to terms with what was
happening.

People left the court in a state of shock,
except for the Wilkins' family who looked
totally unconcerned as they ushered the
distressed servants from the court room. The
Jury left the box and Mary was taken back to
her cell. I glanced at her face as it slipped
into the shadows as she moved further down the
steps into the darkness. The flickering light
of the jailer's candle highlighted the
translucent wetness of her tears.

I felt myself staring at the Judge and I
heard again his crippling words, "Do not think
we are cruel". I wanted to shout at him,
"What on earth did he call cutting of a young
girl in the morning of her day, if not cruelty
of the worst kind?" Yet he shed tears as he
passed the sentence of death upon Mary Morgan.
Why, I wondered, did he need to cry? He
hadn't done so on other occasions. Why now
for this girl? Another nagging doubt for me
to toy with. Mary Morgan was returned to the
jail, together with her three companions in
the dock; they too had been sentenced to
death, but there was no record of George
Hardinge crying for them.

It was over, the ghosts with me in that
court room at Presteigne spirited away as the
voice of the kindly caretaker interrupted my
distant thoughts, "I've brought you a cup of
tea and a Welsh cake". I was glad of the tea,
my mouth was very dry, and as for the Welsh

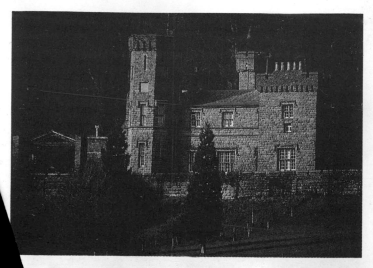

Maesllwych Castle
Glasbury-on-Wye
Photograph by Anita Corbin

's Churchyard, Presteigne
1983
raph by Anita Corbin

cake, that was a bonus. She was well known for her baking was the caretaker of the Shire Hall.

I felt drained after my imaginary ordeal in court but the tea refreshed me as I leaned back and tried to visualise that awful day when they hanged poor Mary.

It was a damp dawn on 13 April 1805, the streets were wet from the night rain; a thunderstorm had hit Presteigne the night before the hanging. The track down Gallows Lane would have been full of puddles and the great tree used for the hangings was no doubt bursting with the new life the spring had brought to its swelling buds.

The Reverend John Harley, Rector of Presteigne, paid his final visit to the condemned girl. He talked to her and advised her to confess her sins and take communion with him. She told him that she thought she had done nothing wrong when she killed her baby and had hoped that her young master would have helped her.

Outside the Shire Hall the cart had not arrived; it is suggested that there had been a dispute with the owner who had refused to drive it, stating that he would not take this girl to the gallows. A driver had to be found from out of town and it was taking some time.

The jailer brought the blacksmith to Mary's cell so that the shackles about her feet could be removed. According to the local stories handed down through generations of Presteignians, Mary was dressed in a long, white, winding sheet, her hands tied at the wrists and she was transported through the town in the open cart.

It is said to have been a quiet procession as it passed my house, so many years ago, on the way to the gallows. It was unlike any other seen in the town before, so it must be fair to assume that no-one approved of, or wanted to see, the execution of Mary Morgan. They took her to the edge of town and tied her to the tree. I was told that she did not die instantly; she was so weak from her long imprisonment, that a man had to be paid one shilling to hang on to her legs to provide the extra weight needed to break her neck.

"Do not think we are cruel." The infamous words from a literary Judge must have stuck in a few throats that April afternoon in 1805. The tenor bell tolled from the tower of St Andrew's Church announcing across the wide spaces of spring that amid its new life there was a death.

Mary Morgan hung from that great tree, the dead victim of a ruthless and corrupt society.

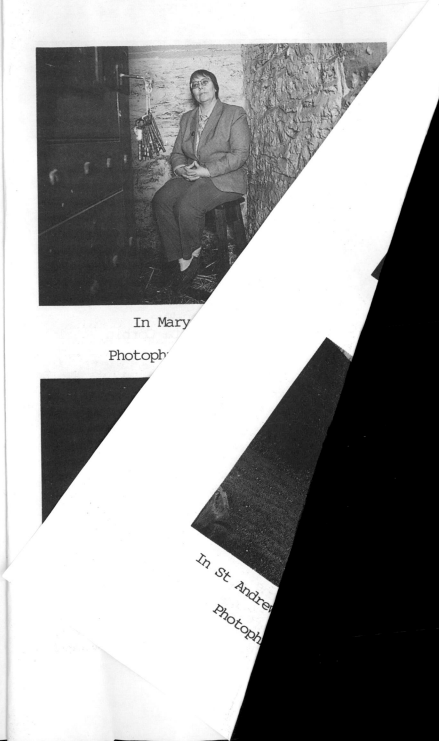

In Mary

Photoph

In St Andre

Photoph

# CHAPTER NINE

## THE AFTERMATH

Presteigne reacted strangely to the execution. Rumours were rife that a man had ridden to London for a reprieve, but records show that none was asked for. It is possible that Sir Samuel Romilly who had connections at Knill Court, close to Presteigne, and was a great social reformer, may have instigated proceedings of that nature.

In the Judges' Chambers at the Shire Hall, the Rector reported that the execution had been carried out and informed Hardinge of his last conversation with the girl before her death. The Wilkins' household would have returned to Glasbury hopeful that the matter would now be forgotten, but not before young Walter had denied everything Mary had said about their relationship.

George Hardinge was very disturbed by the reaction to the death of Mary Morgan and perhaps for good reason. Word was out of the events at Brecon concerning the trial of Mary Morris and comparisons made between the two cases. This must have started the rumour that a man had ridden to London for a reprieve. Hardinge, who would have heard these rumours also, must have had a moment or two of grave concern for his own credibility; he was, after all, the Trial Judge for that case also. He would also have recalled that after the Brecon trial he mounted his horse and rode to Presteigne to hang Mary Morgan. It is a fair assumption that he would have stopped over at Maesllwych (as was his custom on journeys to the Radnorshire Assizes) perhaps discussing both cases with Squire Wilkins and son. Who knows what influences were brought to bear.

It was also clearly recorded that for twenty years previously no female had been sentenced to the death penalty for killing her child soon after its birth. It must have been these factors that encouraged Hardinge to write his intriguing and ambiguous letter to the Bishop of St Asaph; which was interesting enough for John Nichols to include in his 'Illustrations of the Literary History of the Eighteenth Century'. I found it by chance on a visit to the British Museum Library.

I had been advised to read the work of John Nichols if I ever needed background information for a book. It was my intention to read up on Hardinge's own works but I asked the librarian if the Nichols' work was available. It was, all eighteen volumes. I took just one to a reading desk and opened it on the very page showing George Hardinge's letter. I could not shout 'Eureka' in the hallowed confines of the British Museum, although I suppose many of the exhibits have been 'Eurekered' at some time. The excitement inside was uncontainable, no-one to hug this time and if I hadn't got a grip on myself, I might have hugged the librarian! I got out quickly and had a drink in the Museum Tavern, a place that held good memories for me. I then went back and copied out the letter, took it home to Wales and had it typed up. It threw a whole new light on the matter. If George Hardinge wasn't covering his tracks then what was he up to?

"The Right Reverend Dr Horsley,
Lord Bishop of St Asaph

April 1805

My Dear Lord,

With many apologies, and with trembling hope
that you will honour the enclosed with your
attention, I lay them before you and have
nothing more at heart than to obtain a few
hints from you upon so awful and so alarming a
subject. In our part of Wales it is thought
no crime to kill a bastard child. We had two
cases equally desperate. One of the culprits
(and perhaps the worst of the two in a moral
view) escaped. In the case of the girl at
Presteigne, circumstances transpired which are
of a most affecting and peculiar nature. Her
countenance was pretty and modest; it had even
the air and expression of perfect innocence.
Not a tear escaped from her when all around
were deeply affected by her doom; yet her
carriage was respectful, her look attentive,
serious and intelligent. Short as the
interval before she perished, her use of it
was most wonderful. It appeared that she had
no defect of understanding and that she was
born with every disposition to virtue, but of
her crime she had not the faintest conception;
and there was not a single trace of religion
to be found in her thoughts. Of Christianity
she had never even heard, or of the Bible, and
she scarce had ever been at church.
A servant in a most profligate family (she)
attracted the attention of her young master,
who was intrigued with her. Her office was
that of undercook and she killed her child the
moment after its birth with a penknife, nearly
severing the head from the neck. It was the

same knife and the same use of it, which had been her implement and constant habit in killing chickens. This murder it appears by her confession (the most ingenious and complete imaginable) that she committed in mercy to her child. The young Squire, though her favourite gallant, was not the father of the child; but she did him justice in reporting that when he was apprized of her pregnancy he offered to maintain the child when born if she would only say that he was the father. Such was her sense of honour, that although it would have saved her child's life and her own, she would not purchase these two lives with a falsehood.

The father of the child before its birth (admitting the fact) refused in pre-emptory terms to maintain it when born. I determined therefore to kill it, poor thing (she said), out of the way, being perfectly sure that I could not provide for it myself. These were her words and the substance of them was often repeated. Before she was tried, she solicited her young master's help in the gift of a single guinea to her, for a Counsel to do the best for her that he could but her prayer was refused and she would have been undefended if the High Sheriff himself had not, in compassion to her desolate situation, fee'd Counsel himself. She took it for granted that she would be acquitted; had ordered gay apparel to attest her deliverance and supposed the young gentleman (whom I well knew) would save her by a letter to me. She embraced the Gospel Creed and its mercies with enlightened as well as fervent hope; took the sacrament with exemplary devotion; marked a perfect sense of remorse and met her fate in a most affecting manner, with calm intrepidity and with devout resignation. The Minister who attended her told me that a feather of religion would have made an Angel of this girl. To wind up the Characters in this Provincial Tragedy, through to the end of her life she spoke with romantic affection of her young master (whom yet she indirectly accused of seducing her) when she was no more, he gave the lie to all she had asserted and without a shadow of interest. It must not be forgot that her fellow servant, the father of the child, when she complained of her sufferings from pregnancy, gave her a herb which he told her that he had gathered and advised her to take it; which she would never do, believing that it was intended by him to kill her child in her womb. As the law stands, concealment of a pregnancy and birth is punished with two years imprisonment at the most though it is in that concealment that all these murders originate. I have never heard of a Divine, Philosopher, Statesman, Judge, Moralist or even Poet who has written professedly upon this topic. There is, I believe, no allusion to it in Scripture. It never happens in high life, is the vice of the poor, and generally in the pale of domestic servitude. I believe that in every instance of the kind, a total want of religious conceptions or habits will be found one of the features and a neglected education the other. I proportion to the undisciplined and savage characters of the poor, this offence is more or less prevalent.

There has not been a conviction at the Old Bailey for this crime for a period of twenty years and cases of trial for it have been very few. In Wales they have been twice as

numerous and very often fatal. In Ireland I
am told the habit of exposing children to the
elements, most of who die, rages like a
pestilence. I wish to have your Lordship's
opinion how you would correct the law upon
that subject and what expedients you would
recommend for prevention of the mischief. I
will do myself the honour to wait upon you
whenever you will appointment me. It will be
my turn at Brecon to deliver the charge in the
summer; and I wish to do as much good as I
can, by admonition from the bench.
I remain with highest respect my Lord,
Your Grateful and Obedient Servant,
George Hardinge."

In August 1805 George Hardinge commenced his
travels once more, to hold Court at the Welsh
Sessions and he had on his mind his criticism
of the Jury that he was about to face again at
the Brecon Sessions. He had spent some months
thinking about this and had written up, in
advance, the transcript of his reprimand which
had already been circulated to the newspapers
to ensure that everyone knew of his
intentions. It was to be a short Court at
Brecon, just two fellons convicted of the
theft of cattle and trespass. The trial ended
quickly and the Judge addressed the Jury for
the second time that day, reprimanding them
for the acquittal of Mary Morris six months
earlier.
When he got to Presteigne he would have been
surprised to hear that the body of Mary Morgan
had not been sent away to be dissected, but
instead had been taken by the Rector and
buried in his garden and that the local people
had provided a headstone. The words upon it

must surely have hit home hard. Perhaps that is why he had his own words mounted opposite, to counteract any criticism over his actions. Hardinge was never the same man again but he did not learn from his mistakes.

Ten years later, he sentenced another woman, Sarah Chandler, to die at the gallows. She had been charged at Presteigne with changing a one pound note into five pounds and found guilty of forgery; a crime punishable by death. She, too, awaited her execution in the town jail, but this time the people were not going to allow another woman to hang in their town. With the help of the Jailer, who was later dismissed for aiding and abetting the escape, and assisted by her family and friends, Sarah Chandler was broken out of the jail and escaped over the wall with the aid of ladders loaned for the purpose. Hardinge was incensed by what had happened and straight away offered a reward of fifty pounds for her recapture. Almost two years later, she was caught and taken to Portsmouth to await transportation to the Colonies to serve two years in penal servitude.

The effect of his actions in the Mary Morgan case caused George Hardinge much personal suffering. Although there was no official criticism of his decision to hang Mary Morgan, his demeanor became that of a soul confined within a prison of guilt. He was a man in torment and whenever he went to Presteigne, he never failed to attend the grave of the girl he so callously committed to the gallows. He often wrote poems to her memory, and two are included here.

## "ON SEEING THE TOMB OF MARY MORGAN"
### by
### George Hardinge

Flow the tear that pity loves
Upon Mary's hapless fate
It's a tear that God approves,
He can strike, but cannot hate.
Read in time; oh beauteous maid!
Shun the lover's poisoning art
Mary was by love betrayed
And an arrow stung the heart.
Love the constant and the good
Wed the husband of your choice,
Blest is then your children's food,
Sweet the little cherub's voice.
Had religion glanced its beam,
On the mourner's frantic bed,
Mute had been the tablets theme,
Nor would Mary's child have bled.
She, for an example fell,
But is man from censure free?
Thine, seducer is the knell.
It's a messenger, to thee.

The second piece is translated from Latin.

"AN EPITAPH ON MARY MORGAN"
by
George Hardinge

Deserving of our sorrow, let righteousness
prevent our weeping.
She was born into virtue, but lacked religion,
In the flower of her youth, she was corrupt,
a sinful mother, wielding the unholy weapons
of the crime she undertook. She was betrayed,
and the frightened victim of a secret lust,
Hoped not to keep the child she had begun.
Vengence fell upon the witness to her crime,
the child died.
Mary, who deserves our tears, had died, by the
punishment she deserves.
By her death, she has humbly paid the penalty
with modest expression, flying high on the
wings of hope, and strong in her piety.
You women like her, proud in your beauty, weep
for her.
Her ghost, in the shadow warns
Beware of Men.

In the spring of 1816, George Hardinge again arrived on circuit at Presteigne. He had aged considerably over the years and carried his once upright figure with some difficulty. He had a slight chest cold, but this did not prevent him making his accustomed pilgrimage to the grave of Mary Morgan; little did he know it was to be his last. He collapsed, at the graveside of the girl he had treated so badly, and died some days later of pleurisy, at his lodgings in the Old Rectory in St David's Street; well within the sound of the old tenor bell that had tolled for Mary's death eleven years before. It was a sudden and unexpected demise, and his public obituary was an interesting one.

"So various were his powers, that he was a Judge, a Member of Parliament, a poet, a prose writer and a writer of sermons. He occasionally exhibited great eloquence, no-one had a finer choice of words and few, a more graceful delivery. His voice was also sonorous, his imagery rich and classical, his narrative clear and perspicuous. He was possessed of abilities of the highest order and great expectations were formed as to his career in the legal profession, but his natural indolence, blended with his intense desire for literary success, doomed him to failure."

The legacy he left behind him was a miscellaneous collection of his literary works and an undelivered speech that should have been presented to the Jury at Presteigne, had not his untimely death intervened. This speech was yet again concerned with his decision regarding Mary Morgan. How strange that he should still be so concerned about it eleven years later.

George Hardinge also left behind him an unexplained miscarriage of justice that has lain dormant in the annals of Welsh legal history. It appears that he was obsessed with the guilt of his discredited actions, which must surely have haunted him in the declining years of his profitable life. Why so eminent a legal personage became so intertwined with the life and death of a very young, unimportant servant girl remains a secret that lies with the dust of his bones in some unknown burial ground.

The story of the trial of Mary Morgan became a talking point throughout the whole of Mid Wales and the Border Counties, even reaching as far afield as Birmingham, Manchester and London. Whenever people came to Presteigne, they talked with the local people about the case.

In the summer of 1818, Mr Waldergrave's Company of actors, on a tour of the Borderland, came to perform and entertain in the town. A member of this troupe of strolling players was a comedian, by the name of T Horton. So taken was he with the story and the gravestones that some say he was never funny again. He was inspired to write a long poem, which was then produced and printed up in a small booklet entitled:

AN ELEGY
Written in a Country Churchyard
at Presteigne, Radnorshire
with admonitory reflections
on
The Grave of
MARY MORGAN
Who was interred there, after suffering
the awful sentence of the law for
the murder of her illegitimate child.
by
T Horton, Comedian

who respectfully inscribes this little work to
those:
"Whose breasts with generous pity deign
    to glow,
For human frailty, or for human woe,
Who do not blush to ope' misfortunes
    door.
Or scorn the simple annals of the poor."

Horton precedes his poetic words with the
following announcement:
"The author of this little poem, under
a deep sense of gratitude from the
distinguished patronage he has been
honoured with by those ladies and
gentlemen who perused the manuscript and
by whose example so respectable and
numerous a list of subscribers follows,
in presenting it to the public eye,
humbly hopes its errors may be forgiven,
when he assures them it was written with
an intention to a moral to Young Females
in the same sphere of life in which poor
Mary Morgan moved and, by her fate, to
warn them of the dreadful consequences a

single deviation from the path of virtue
may ultimately lead to.
   If that his lines will prove a means
      to save,
   But one fair reader from an untimely
      grave,
   If they but shield from sorrow, sin
      and shame,
   Though weak the verse immortal were
      its fame."

"ELEGY TO MARY MORGAN"
by
T HORTON
COMEDIAN

Stay, gentle passenger, and pause awhile,
Nor fear these silent mansions of the dead;
Where lie releas'd from every pain and toil,
Departed friends within their narrow bed.
Behold these monuments of life's frail lease,
Mortality's sad emblems scattered round,
Proclaiming where at rest beneath in peace;
Repose the tenants of this hallow'd ground.
Here haughty pride's compell'd to lower his
   crest,
Here spurned merit finds a safe retreat,
Here infant innocence reclines at rest,
Within the sepulchre beneath our feet.
But lo behold, yon solitary stone,
Modest it rears its russet colour'd head,
As if at humble distance it was thrown,
Denied communion with the kindred dead.
Approach it, passenger, and do not scorn
The memorial inscrib'd upon its face;
The awful fate of a poor maid forlorn,
With feeling heart, and tearful eye thou'lt
   trace.

115

POOR MARY, who beneath this stone is laid,
Who once a virtuous, lovely, village maid,
Humble in birth, among her kindred poor,
Meek as the daisy, as the daisy pure;
Which in the meadow from its grassy bed,
Smiles to the morn, just tip'd with modest
  red;
Sweet as the vernal moon's nocturnal beam,
Sweet as the sunshine sparkling on the stream.
Belove'd and happy in her sphere she shone,
Esteem'd by all, her artless manners won;
Blooming in years, with modest grace attir'd,
By age respected, and by youth admired,
Admir'd! Alas! How shall the muse disclose
The cause of Mary's end, of Mary's woes;
She like another maid, whose hapless fate
In every breast a sorrow does create.
Poor MARY ASHFORD, hapless, murder'd maid,
With every modest beauteous grace array'd
By barbarous man deprived of virtue bright,
Then hurl'd confounded, to the realms of
  night.
Dreadful indeed, tho' blessed was her doom,
To thine, poor sleeper, in this silent tomb;
By treacherous man, indeed she was destroy'd,
But still her heart to guilt was unallied:
Not so thy lot, by faithless man deceiv'd,
And all his flattering promises believ'd
Thy innocence and spotless fame resign'd
And all the comforts of sweet peace of mind.
Then fell remorse with all his haggard train,
Seiz'd pure honour from its downy nest,
And fill'd with sorrow's pangs, thy troubled
  breast;
Whose barbed arrow piercing to the heart,
Affrighted peace, and bid her to depart;
For peace with guilty minds can never dwell,
She scorns deception's charm, or vice's cell.

116

In vain was every effort to retrace,
The steps that led thee to thy sad disgrace,
Which to conceal from each suspecting eye,
And shun the opprobrious name of infamy.
The tempter, Satan, enemy to joy,
Bade thee, the fruits thy folly made, destroy;
Bade thee forbid the vital spark to glow,
Forbid the crimson flood of life to flow.
Taught thy poor heart another crime to know,
And whisper'd Murder to complete thy woe.
No longer under virtue's strict control,
And horror seizing on thy trembling soul,
The deed was done, the tempter's conquest
   gain'd,
Whilst thou to sad despair, a prey remain'd
But nature anxious in her children's cause,
Sought satisfaction from the injur'd laws,
And justice, strict impartial justice came,
To prove her right, and to enforce her claim:
Tho' by her side, sweet mercy trembling stood,
Blood! she exclaim'd, must be repaid by blood!
Poor hapless frail one, lo thy judge appears,
Cloth'd with respected venerable years,
The sage experience dwelt within his breast,
Where pity sat to feel for the distressed.
Thy case, alas! his anxious bosom mov'd
For though to justice dear, he mercy lov'd;
Strove all his power, thy acquittal to obtain,
But, Oh! (sad truth) alas, he strove in vain!
With heavy heart did he pronounce the doom,
Which sentenc'd thee to an untimely tomb;
And oft upon thy melancholy bear,
He's dropped the tribute of a friendly tear.
Much pitied maid, could none thy life prolong!
Not one thy advocate amid the throng?
Yes urg'd by charity thy life to save,
And snatch thee from a malefactor's grave.
Many humanely strove thy cause to plead,

But oh! in vain, for justice had decreed,
The awful sentence of the law was past,
And this world's destiny of lot was cast;
And every one who knew thy hapless name,
Wept o'er the victim of remorse and shame:
And pray'd that tho' in this court unforgiven,
Eternal mercy, thou might'st find in heaven!
Where sinners, penitent in God who trust,
Receive the welcome greetings of the just.
Poor child of error, this we trust's thy lot,
Preach to thy soul, and be thy faults forgot;
And oh, ye maids who tread life's vernal
    plain,
From Mary's sad example knowledge gain.
To shun the poison of a flatt'ring tongue.
Nor listen to the gay fantastic song,
Which vice and folly echo through the air,
Too oft the ruin of the heedless fair.
But wisdom's ways of pleasure strict pursue,
And keep Religion ever in your view;
Be hope the mild conductress of your way,
Nor ever from the paths of prudence stray:
Blest with such guides, you'll merit earth's
    regard,
And when you quit it, find in heav'n reward.
Be not afraid to visit Mary's tomb,
Or drop a pitying tear upon her doom;
And ever as you do her stone survey,
Hope, that her suff'rings wash'd her sins away.

*****

And that, you may think, should be the end
of the story; a poetic finish to the saga of
Mary Morgan. After all the research, all the
discovery, there was no stone left to unturn,
the secret secret of Presteigne remained just
that - but it still bothered me. So much

118

material to play with, so many questions left
unanswered, so many emotions I had to come to
terms with and, overiding it all, my spiritual
friendship with a dead girl. The struggle
wasn't over yet; I knew I had to find myself
before I could find her. It was going to be a
long confinement and my labours painful. Mary
was in my system and I had to deliver her,
clean and wholesome, to a waiting modern day
Presteigne, part of which was anxious for me
to come unstuck in the process.

CHAPTER TEN

THE VERDICT


The battle was on. It seemed like me
against the world; a world of books, public
records, newspaper cuttings, historians past
and present. It was me having to take on the
ghosts of the Wilkins family, the Judge and a
small Welsh border town. This was a town that
I cared about, lived in and somewhere along
the way, got lost in. A town where some people
couldn't come to terms with a past of myth and
hearsay and who were ready to ostracise me,
should I cast a pebble into their still pool.

But on my side, to fight with me, against
all the odds, I had Mary Morgan. I believed
in her and she in me. Together we win,
divided . . . well, we are not divisible and
whatever emotional cracks appeared in my life
I closed them up again and got on with it.

I now had the fact and the fiction, passed
down through books and papers in various
libraries throughout England and Wales. Tales
handed down from mother to daughter with moral
intent, father to son with a more chauvinistic
leaning, from the doubting Thomas's who saw
Mary as a "wicked, wicked woman" and from
those for whom she had become an unsung
heroine.

Mary Morgan should not have stood trial for
murder that day. She took upon her frail
shoulders the crimes of an uncaring society,
the sins of the upper classes and the
innocence of her youth. She carried to her
lonely grave the name of the father of her
dead child and, I believe, so too did Walter

Wilkins Senior, his son and Mr Justice George Hardinge, plus one or two other members of those twelve 'just men and true' who so readily acclaimed "Guilty of murder".

Ponder this! Why did such an esteemed Judge become so emotional about a sentence he often passed and was noted for? Why the ambiguities of his letter to a Bishop? Why the passing of a sentence of death so uncommon as to be rare? Why did past historians deviate from the fact? What was there to hide that was awful enough to send a girl, barely seventeen years old, to such a cruel end and has left a town still privately mourning almost two hundred years on?

Someone still cares. A town still cares. Although it won't speak for itself, in its own quiet way it will forever respect the memory of the young Welsh girl it could not save from the gallows.

Mary Morgan lies in concecrated ground now, brought about by the inclusion of the rectory garden into the churchyard during the nineteenth century. At Christmas time a wreath of holly is placed on her grave and on 13 April, every year, bright daffodils are left for her; a custom passed down through the generations of Presteigne. It doesn't matter who does it, it only matters that somebody takes the trouble to leave a splash of bright colour, shining out of the grey and green landscape and laid at the base of the small gravestone. Who knows! Perhaps it's the bouquet of guilt, that hides in its floral arrangement the responsibility of a class system that executed a young woman, more sinned against than sinning, an employer who cared little for anything but his 'good name', a Judge who bent the rules and a society that did not care.

It is to the eternal credit of Presteigne that it erected its own tribute, placed there to contradict that of a hypocritical Judge and serve as a reminder to us all; past, present and future:

"He that is without sin among you,
Let him first cast the stone at her."

Could the long lost, secret secret of Presteigne be hidden in those words? Words not passed down by sight and sound, nor incomers and passers by, but inherently preserved by the indigenous population of Presteigne. Simple words on a headstone, that have been nurtured through the decades and altered at some point, because a closer look will show that the word 'suffered' has been engraved over an earlier one; probably in place of 'hanged'.

The time had come to gather my papers and my thoughts and attempt to put them all together. Where to begin and how to do it, that was the big question. My only writing experience was of pantomimes. This was no pantomime, but I would have a go at dramatising the story. Good God! How arrogant, a non-academic, eleven-plus failure, writing a play; I could feel the smirks beginning to form on the faces of my peers. Sod 'em! I had to have a go at something.

Financially, things weren't too good. The Coffee Pot was just about scraping by, the Happy Nut (that's me) wasn't. Garden Cottage had been sold and my friend was about to make a new start elsewhere and withdraw from my life. This was a hard fact to face after almost a decade of friendship; it hurt, but you shouldn't let hurt linger too long when life is full of doors waiting to be opened. Some day I would open the right one. I missed her, but I had other friends to fill the space she left and I still had Mary Morgan to dwell upon.

It took me two weeks, working between six and twelve in the evening, to commit my story to paper and I did so without pause and without tearing up one sheet. It just flowed out of me, and came together in a rough sort of way. The joy of my personal achievement spilled into the earth that covered Mary, as I ran to the churchyard to tell her I had done it. It must have been a peculiar sight to anyone who saw me, skipping through a graveyard, after midnight, and smiling broadly. I truly was the 'Happy Nut'.

Was this, then, the literary beginning at the end of a historical quest, or should I take the easy way out? Pack up my papers, call it a day and beetle off back to 'suburbia'; the land of the living not the dead. After all, I was emotionally battered, financially broke and on the way to taking a beating. But that still small voice kept nagging away inside my head. "Stay with it", it seemed to say, and I am a stayer.

My long time companion had gone and I had to adjust to living alone, which was a very hard re-adjustment for one of six children, who moved out of a close family life straight into communal living in the Women's Royal Naval Service, onto sharing London flats with friends and then one to one relationships. But it got easier, I was getting stronger; something, or someone, was giving me inner strengths I never knew I had. Friends and family were a great help and my mother, quietly supportive in her own special way, was a joy in my life, despite the distance between us. Presteigne, also, wrapped its warmth around me, albeit for a limited period. I began to enjoy the creative space being alone gave me; I was finding myself at last.

There were shows to write and direct for the "Entertainers", Council meetings to go to (I had, by now, become "Councillor Ms Green", although they never could get the 'Ms' right) and Royal Wedding street parties to attend; which constantly reminded me of Mary Morgan and the 'fairs, functions and entertainers' that filled up her short life. I was back into it again.

The conversation in the Coffee Pot once more began to centre around my researches, new snippets of information filtering through, and I soon realised that this story wasn't over yet. The play I had written lay idle in a drawer, accompanied by a clutch of rejection slips, helpful letters and kind words. Well, it was a bit presumptuous to send it to the Royal Shakespeare Company, but starting at the top seemed the right thing to do at the time, but where did I go from there?

Well, I went to a party. It was a preview of an exhibition of paintings held at the gallery of the late Lady Rennell of the Rod, near Presteigne. The artist was living locally and I was acquainted with her, but not her work. It turned out to be an eventful night. There was food, wine, pictures, good company and a man called Clem, who was a friend of the artist. He had links with television and we talked long about the Welsh Border country and Presteigne. He asked me if anything exciting ever happened there and I told him something did in 1805. My roller coaster of a mind churned it all out. He was really taken up with the story and said it would make a great television play. I told him I had written one, and he advised me to send it to an independent film maker he knew who had leanings towards the feminist movement. Clem felt that Sarah would have an affinity with my feelings and even if she wasn't interested in the project herself, she would work hard on my behalf to get the story told. I noted down her address and got on with the party.

The following day I realised the party was really over and I had to get on with Mary's life and my own. A bank statement confirmed I was going broke. I closed my shop, remortgaged the property, enough to pay the debts, and posted off my creative package. I needed a job and became Warden of Dowdell Hall at the Royal National College for the Visually Handicapped in Hereford. Living away from my home plus the unsocial hours were easily compensated for by the free time I had in the day in which to write, and the long holidays to linger over in Presteigne. An added benefit was the good feelings of being involved with the realities of life again and the growing awareness that I was slowly breaking the bonds that bound me to Presteigne; although there was a still a long way to go.

I'm still at the College and the bank smiles upon me once more. From time to time, I would mull over all my researches and wait for little bits of the Mary Morgan jigsaw puzzle to break through the routine and challenge me again.

On a premature Spring day in 1982, Jack Crutchley died. Jack was a retired postman, Presteigne born and bred, who became a special friend during my early days in the town. He had many stories to tell, many anecdotes to quote, but rarely would he talk of Mary Morgan, save to say, "It was a tragedy what happened to the poor girl". I would often try to open up a discussion with him, but he could not be persuaded to chat about her.

It was about 6.00 pm in the evening when I last spoke with him. He was ambling to his Broad Street cottage and came to sit next to me, on the wrought iron seat by the churchyard gate. We commented upon the weather and the town, and he stressed how much he had enjoyed his life in Presteigne. He died unexpectedly later that evening, having gone beyond his three score years and ten.

A well attended funeral service was held in St Andrew's, but few went to the cemetery for the internment; the cemetery being across the border in England. We gathered round his final resting place: the Rector, Jack's sister, his niece, plus a friend from a farm out of town and me. The sun shone, but it was a cold wind that rushed through the hedge as I stooped to pick a solitary primrose. I dropped it onto the plain wooden coffin and it landed beside the brass name plate that read, 'John Hardinge Crutchley'.

Hardinge - the name of the Judge - had cropped up again, 166 years after his death in 1816, at the funeral of a simple postman. The shock almost caused me to fall into the grave myself, but I recovered enough to ask Jack's sister about the middle name. All she said was, "It was father's and fathers before". Strange he would not talk about Mary Morgan. What little bit of history did Jack Crutchley take to his grave?

Some years later, whilst giving a talk about my researches to a group of people in Luton, I related this interesting coincidence. A woman at the gathering interrupted and said, "You know the primrose is the flower of deceit?". No, I didn't know . . .

It was talking to Mrs Parkin that did it. She was in her eighties, and came for tea one afternoon. We chatted about her childhood and how she wasn't allowed to look at Mary's grave because the word 'bastard' was engraved upon the stone. I asked her about the reprieve; had a man really ridden to London? I had checked the records but there was nothing to support the claim. But Mrs Parkin told a slightly different version. A man had ridden to London for a pardon but his horse cast a shoe at Byton, about three miles from town, and he never got back in time. It was the stuff stories are made of, but it couldn't be true - could it?

Now a pardon is different from a reprieve. The reprieve is asked for in mercy to the guilty, a pardon is usually asked for in cases of irregularities in proceedings. So I asked Mrs Parkin, "Why a pardon?" "Well", she said, "They sent for the pardon on the grounds of a miscarriage of justice. They did say that the Judge was the father of the child".

All hell let loose in my mind. The Judge, the father of the child! Well, he did cry on passing sentence, he did know the Wilkins, he

127

did write poetry to her and he did visit the grave twice a year. One newspaper, dated around the turn of the century, stated quite clearly that, "Her benevolent Judge refrained from exercising his power to delay the execution, beyond the then customary period of forty-eight hours from the sentence being passed, and thereby rendered the obtaining of a reprieve almost an impossibility". One hundred and fifty-two miles to London, on horse-back in two days, a round trip of over three hundred miles. What a stone to unturn, and what a great big piece of my jigsaw puzzle. If this was true, what a way to get rid of the principal witness!

I was after him like the proverbial dog goes after the rabbit and I wasn't going to let go. Box files were opened up, statements studied and research notes re-read over and over again. I decided that the letter to the Bishop of St Asaph was a bit of a buck passer; blame for the pregnancy landing at every door-step but his own, the pertinent knock at the Wilkins' way of life and not a very clear understanding of how he stood on the matter.

George Hardinge had the opportunity to liaise with young Mary; he often stayed at Maesllwych, he liked the ladies but had no natural children of his own. If it was his child then it would allow his tears to fall for his dead daughter and justify his decision to hang the murdering mother. But was it? Judge Hardinge went on circuit into Wales twice a year in April and September. Mary would have had to become impregnated in January to have delivered her child in September. It would have been a long, cold ride to Glasbury just to dally with a servant girl. Even allowing for a premature birth George Hardinge has an alibi. Another myth bites the dust.

I began putting back the notes and records, but with no sense of urgency, while I drank coffee and dawdled with the time. A newspaper cutting caught my attention; it was the one that had been secretly pushed under my door, one misty autumn night. It was a whole page devoted to a tourist's eye view of the town of Presteigne, listing the many attractions available to the visitor. The page was undated, but judging by the style of print and paper and the advertisements, it appeared to be about twenty-five years old. I browsed through it again, this time looking for a clue rather than background; the basis on which I had half-heartedly perused it before. A half column was all that was given to Mary Morgan's case, but a few inches in that column renewed my flagging interest. It reiterated a sentence I had seen in a cutting from a newspaper issued at the turn of the century, which referred to "the instrument of destruction being supplied by the father of the murdered child". This report went even further; it clearly stated, "The father of the child, who was a well-to-do local man, not only urged her to kill the child and gave her a penknife to do it with, but also sat upon the Grand Jury that returned a true bill against her". It may be just another case of literary licence but, for this amateur historical sleuth, the bells rang as the final piece of my jigsaw puzzle slotted into place.

It could only be Walter Wilkins Junior, the young master of whom Mary had "indirectly accused of seducing her". He was well-to-do, he did have easy access to her and, most likely, would have carried a penknife with which to sharpen his quills. He did promise to pay for her defence (although he later denied this) and he was on the Grand Jury.

But did it really matter? It was usual for servant girls to be used and abused by the males of the household. In some families the household looked after its own and pregnant girls were taken care of. Mary was 'taken care of' all right, because the Wilkins were not the old established gentry; they were the 'nouveau riche'. They were the jumped-up middle classes of the eighteenth century, completely unaware of how to behave in such circumstances, and not wanting their newly acquired status disturbed. So the 'Nabob of Glasbury' jumped in with both feet and sank any dog's chance Mary might have had. But why hang her? I have thought about it for a long time now, almost ten years, and I always come to the same conclusion.

Young Walter had the opportunity to give her the knife, but did he have the motive? I think he did. Having seduced the girl and finding himself the father of an unwanted child, he realised that it would interfere with all his father's plans for him. His marriage into the Hereford line, his position in Society, all prompted him to try to get out of the situation without causing his ambitious father to over react.

On the other hand, he did, for some reason, want a child (that's if the Judge's words are to be believed) and he told Mary he would maintain the child if only she would say it was his; a statement he later denied. So the young man takes his pleasures, but does not intend to pay for them with his future. He had obviously communicated his feelings to Mary at some point, perhaps he even told his father that he did care for the girl, but profligate Squire Wilkins was having none of it. It is likely he told his son and heir to do what he had to do and get rid of the girl and her child. It was, after all, common place to kill your unwanted child, and have the murder charge dropped and replaced by a charge of not registering the birth; punished only by a custodial sentence. Thus Mary killed the baby, knowing that she would be acquitted of murder and with the promised support of her young master and lover, she would be freed.

All was well until young Walter gave her the knife with which to carry out the killing. That is where he made his mistake, because if he did provide the weapon then he would surely have become an accessory to the fact and would have been tried, alongside Mary Morgan, for the premeditated murder of the bastard child.

Was this, then, the turning point in Mary's life. If these facts had become common knowledge surely a defender would have had a case to take before the Court, thus having a domino effect on the well planned future of the Wilkins family. But Walter Wilkins Senior had a friend at Court, legal court that is. How very fortuitous that Mr Justice George Hardinge MP, Honourable Judge for the Counties of Glamorgan, Brecon and Radnor was on circuit that month and on his way through Glasbury. Lucky Walter, unlucky Mary! "Gentry always sticks together".

Why then, didn't Mary tell her story in Court? Defendants were not allowed to speak for themselves and her defender, appointed a few hours before the trial commenced, (he would have rode in with the Judge) would have had little or no time with her. Mary was quite certain that her young master would see her through the ordeal and arrange for her acquittal. So she went through the trial, apparently quite unconcerned, dressed in bright clothes and confident that Walter would 'get her off' by sending a letter to the Judge. Hence the fact that 'not a tear escaped her, when all around were deeply affected by her doom'. It was no use her crying 'foul play' after sentence had been passed.

Everyone knew, except naive young Mary, that she was being set up, swept under the carpet, to protect the family Wilkins. The townsfolk knew. Her fellow servants, with their almost identical statements signed with a cross, knew and, you can bet your life, the nineteenth century media knew; gagged of course by the power of Wilkins Senior.

And Hardinge knew they knew. That's why he shed his tears, wrote his poems and spent the rest of his days under a cloud of guilt, emphasising his true feelings in the last line of one of his poems, "You women like her, proud in your beauty, weep for her. Her ghost in the shadow warns, Beware of Men".

That, then, rightly or wrongly, is my theory and I am sticking to it. Mary knows I'm right because when I went back to the churchyard to tell her, her presence was even stronger. The cool, evening breeze that floated on the night air, brushed through the overhanging branches of the trees and created a sigh of satisfaction, passed from her to me.

I knew then my mission was almost complete and all that was left was to write it all up and leave, but there was still the tail end of my journey through time to come to terms with.

# CHAPTER ELEVEN

## THE ENDING

In the summer of 1982, I came home from College and made my customary call upon Mary Morgan, only to find that the large headstone had been removed and placed inside the church; much to the dismay of the locals and to me. The Rector, relatively new to Presteigne, had also become taken up with the plight of poor Mary and, with kind intent, felt that the large headstone was decidedly in need of care and protection. It had been savaged by harsh winters and he had been advised by an expert in stone work that the life span of the stone would be considerably shortened if it remained outside. So, in consultation with the Parochial Church Council, it was to be taken into the church and laid up for safekeeping and, after obtaining a faculty from the Bishop, it was fixed to the church wall, on view for all to see, for ever and a day.

"Oh no!" the town's people exclaimed. "Oh yes!" responded the power of the Church and the town was split once more, over a dead girl. The breach was healed when, some weeks later, persons unknown retrieved the heavy stone from inside the church and returned it to its rightful place. During the hours of darkness it was well and truly cemented into the ground, never to be removed again.

Eventually, the press got to hear about it and I was asked for my comments. The saga of Mary Morgan was extracted from me and, as usual with the media, they highlighted the curse and not the incident. "Jenny Fights The

Curse of Mary Morgan" the local paper acclaimed and the whole town had a wobbly. The snipers came out, close friends and old Presteignians threw a cordon around me and the flak died down, but not for long. The BBC Radio invited me to make a programme about my researches which, although very successful for them, rocked my boat so hard that it all but turned turtle, and I almost ran for my life. It wasn't so much the story that upset the town, but the fact that the reporter described it as the "ultimate British backwater with signs of Transylvania". It was a heavy description for that pretty little town, but to the casual stranger on a cold autumn night . . . well allowances have to be made. Strange to relate though that, shortly after the broadcast went out in 1983, the same reporter had an unexplained car crash, in which he and his wife were seriously injured.

The after effects of the broadcast were considerable and very few people would speak to me. A rival drama group formed, who wrote and performed a play about the broadcast and I took some stick. Even the now-retired caretaker of the Shire Hall, who had been so kind to me, cut me dead because she was absolutely convinced that Mary did not cut her baby's throat and I was making it all up.

Many people thought I was in it for the money. What money?! It had cost me my savings, my business, my relationships and, at times, my peace of mind. I think the last straw was to be told I would be forced out of the town within twelve months, and for weeks I felt very threatened by a town to which I had given a lot in many ways.

I still had a few loyal supporters left, the real people of Presteigne who knew I was right to do what I had to do. There was the former 'Coffee Pot Groupies' who still had time for me, and whose good humour kept me going on the bad days, and I can never forget the close friends, near and far, who would wrap me with their love and affection and keep me warm when the chill of fear and failure occasionally trickled through my veins. They would pick up my pieces, glue me back together again and put me back in the ring to fight another day. You see, I have the blessing of Mary Morgan, not the curse, to watch over me.

Later that year I lost my greatest friend and my biggest fan; my mother died. The frailty of her declining years caught up with her during a September weekend, the same weekend some 180 years previous that Mary Morgan had killed her child. On the Saturday afternoon, as some of her children, grandchildren and great grandchildren gathered round her hospital bed, Radio Four was repeating my story, "Poor Mary Who Beneath This Stone". It was ironic really I suppose, that just as my mother was dying, her much loved daughter was resurrecting Mary Morgan. I stayed with my mother for almost two days, holding her hand until she reached her promised land, and when, in her last moment on this good earth, I asked her to give me a smile before she left me, I rejoiced in the knowledge that she heard and did. How glad I felt, that she had chosen to leave on a sunfilled autumn day, that left me knowing that my joy of life, love and sense of humour had been inherited from such a stoical and wonderful working class woman. How fortunate I was to be one of her six children.

Shortly after this major setback to my life, the Rector of Presteigne 'did it again'. For some bizarre reason, he decided to hold a 'Service of Restitution' which he had personally devised, to pray for the soul of all those connected with the case of Mary Morgan. It felt uncannily like exorcism to me. I was uneasy as I stood at the graveside, watching the service with the other twenty or so people in attendance. I needn't have done. I could almost see Mary's amused smile hovering between the gravestones as the prayers were said over her, forgiving her for her sins! I managed to get some film of it, hopefully to use in any drama/documentary that one day may be produced.

Still I pressed on, looking for clues to add to my growing researches. I even went back to Glasbury to see the castle and stop for tea at The Oaklands Women's Centre in the village. I had been aware of it for many years, little knowing the final connection it had with Mary Morgan. The centre is based in a large old house in the village and on the hillside, behind it, is Maesllwych Castle; still occupied by a Wilkins/De Winton. Oaklands was donated by a woman to the London Women's Liberation Workshop for use as a holiday retreat for battered women and their children. A nice idea. It was only by chance that I discovered that the donor appears to be none other than Emily De Winton, great, great, great, great grand-daughter of young Walter Wilkins. She won't talk to me about it, despite her feminist leanings, but how interesting that the female descendant of the

137

possible father of Mary Morgan's bastard
child, gave her inheritance to be used as a
holiday home for battered women and their
children. I wonder if her middle name is
Mary.

The long and winding road that leads to
Presteigne is no more. They've built a by-
pass, courtesy of the EEC, but I'm leaving the
way I came in. My possessions have gone on
ahead, but my memories are carried inside me.

I went back to the churchyard to say goodbye
and her presence was still all around me, but
a much happier presence. The dying daffodils
on the gravestone told me that someone will
always care and I left her safe in that
knowledge. But I knew, deep inside my soul,
that I was only leaving her physically and not
spiritually, and that our friendship is
intransient. Just as I have looked out for
her, I know she will always look out for me.

I shall constantly ask myself, "Why me"? Of
all the people who have trod the pathway to
her grave, for almost two hundred years, why
did she choose me to try to clear her name?
Only Mary knows the answer and one day she
will tell me why; that will be my secret
secret.

I locked the door to my little house for the
very last time and posted the key through the
letter box, for the new owner. Ginge was
again in the back of the car, Tabby had
returned to Garden Cottage to die among the
raspberry canes he loved so much.

Not a soul was about as I left the town that
had taken almost a quarter of my life from me
and dissected my emotions, pinning them down
like the wings of a captured butterfly. One

day I'm going to fly again, so high that no-one can reach me. I'll drift through time, and recall my meeting with a seventeen year old servant girl who "dreamed that love was divine and a foretaste to heaven and who awoke to find it the road to perdition" and the gateway to her death. Her young life, cut off in the morning of her day.

I left Presteigne through the Hereford end and I knew it was the town, and not me, that was lost. At The Bell at Byton I turned for one last look at the place where I had become so caught up in a provincial tragedy that captured a small Welsh border town. It was still there.

# THE EPILOGUE

I'm back in the Home Counties again on familiar ground and sharing my days between London and Somerset, but I'm still under the spell of Mary Morgan. She still dogs my tracks and as the coincidences continue I am constantly reminded of our journey through time.

While I was writing my book I was introduced to a man who was visiting Hereford. The friend he had come to see was unable to spend any time with him that day and I was asked to look after him. The visitor was an English artist who lives in America where he holds exhibitions of his work and writes books about American painters. Over lunch, and later tea, we talked endlessly about Mary Morgan and his interest and enthusiasm for the story was so encouraging.

We were sitting on the platform at Hereford railway station awaiting his train to London when he suggested that my story would make a good film and promised that when he got back to America he would try to raise the capital to make it happen. We said goodbye and I never gave the idea another serious thought, yet I felt sure that we would meet up again one day. Four years later he wrote to me and told me he was coming to London and wanted to talk about the Mary Morgan story. He came, we met and plans were made, and it was then I discovered that he shared the same birthday as Mary. A film treatment has since been developed and the research goes on and on.

During this period a small theatre company staged a potted version of the story, but decided to change the ending slightly. In the event, the opening night had to be put back because of a fire in their rehearsal rooms and then a little later one of the cast became pregnant. How strange that the expected birth date was 23 September; the same day as Mary Morgan had had her child.

Eventually, I moved to London to take up a post as Warden of Walsingham Lodge, a group of Alms Houses in Barnes. Just a few miles away was Ragmans Castle, the former home of Judge George Hardinge. I came across it quite by chance, while I was driving to an appointment. It stood in a lay-by, just off a busy road, and it was an eerie moment as I turned and drove up to the house because I had the distinct feeling that he was going to appear in the doorway and ask me in. So you see, she is still about me, nudging me along the pathway.

These days, I am surrounded by Morgans. I have a friend called Morgan and a poser of a cat, also called Morgan, and when I manage to slip away to my home in Somerset for a period of peaceful creativity what do I discover in the local history books? There is a house in Frome where, in the middle of the 19th Century, a "Mrs Morgan was supposed murdered". Now that's another story . . . or is it?

## ACKNOWLEDGEMENTS

The author is very grateful to The Pilkington Department of Business Studies at the Royal National College for the Blind for their practical help. In particular, I thank Margaret Tennant and Jane Lilleystone for their continued support.

Thank you to Pauline Richardson, a past student of the College, and her guide dog Irma, for the patience they both showed during the long hours we spent compiling the initial researches.

To my friends Joan Roberts, Christine Williams and Sarah Boston for believing I could do it.

Special thanks to my Editor, Christine Morgan, without whom my story may never have become a reality.

Finally, thank you to the town and people of Presteigne for just being there.

BIBLIOGRAPHY

'A History of the English People in the 19th Century' Elie Halevy. Translated from the French by E I Watkins and D A Baker.
'A General History of the County of Radnor' The Reverand John Williams.
'Illustrations of the Literary History of the 19th Century' John Nichols.
'Welsh Life in the 18th Century' Davis and Edwards,
'The Miscellaneous Works of George Hardinge'
'Peacocks in Paradise' Elizabeth Inglis-Jones.
'A Welsh Border Town' and 'Presteigne Past and Present' W H Howse.
'History of India' P Spear.
'Robert Clive' Richard Garrett
'The Life of Wilberforce'
'The Nabobs' from the Indian Civil Service
'The Philanthropists'
'Burkes Peerage and Landed Gentry'
'The Dictionary of National Biography'
'The Cambrian', 'The Salopian', 'The Hereford Journal', 'The Shrewsbury Chronicle', 'The Penzance Examiner', 'The Birmingham Post', 'The Western Mail'.
'The National Library of Wales' (Ancient Manuscripts and Records Department)
'The British Library'
'The Hereford City Library'